THE
Real
TOLTEC
PROPHECIES

ALSO BY SERGIO MAGAÑA

Caves of Power (Hay House, 2016)

The Toltec Secret (Hay House, 2014)

2012–2021: The Dawn of the Sixth Sun
(Edizioni Amrita, 2011; Blossoming Books, 2012)

THE

Real

TOLTEC
PROPHECIES

How the Aztec Calendar Predicted
Modern-Day Events and Reveals a
Pathway to a New Era of Humankind

SERGIO MAGAÑA

HAY HOUSE

Carlsbad, California • New York City
London • Sydney • New Delhi

Published in the United Kingdom by:
Hay House UK Ltd, The Sixth Floor, Watson House
54 Baker Street, London W1U 7BU
Tel: +44 (0)20 3927 7290; Fax: +44 (0)20 3927 7291; www.hayhouse.co.uk

Published in the United States of America by:
Hay House Inc., PO Box 5100, Carlsbad, CA 92018-5100
Tel: (1) 760 431 7695 or (800) 654 5126
Fax: (1) 760 431 6948 or (800) 650 5115; www.hayhouse.com

Published in Australia by:
Hay House Australia Ltd, 18/36 Ralph St, Alexandria NSW 2015
Tel: (61) 2 9669 4299; Fax: (61) 2 9669 4144; www.hayhouse.com.au

Published in India by:
Hay House Publishers India, Muskaan Complex,
Plot No.3, B-2, Vasant Kunj, New Delhi 110 070
Tel: (91) 11 4176 1620; Fax: (91) 11 4176 1630; www.hayhouse.co.in

Text © Sergio Magaña, 2020

The moral rights of the author have been asserted.

The information given in this book should not be treated as a substitute for professional medical advice; always consult a medical practitioner. Any use of information in this book is at the reader's discretion and risk. Neither the author nor the publisher can be held responsible for any loss, claim or damage arising out of the use, or misuse, of the suggestions made, the failure to take medical advice or for any material on third-party websites.

A catalogue record for this book is available from the British Library.

Tradepaper ISBN: 978-1-4019-6271-5
E-book ISBN: 978-1-78817-570-8
Audiobook ISBN: 978-1-78817-586-9

Interior images: vii, ix, xi, xix, 1, 19, 43, 55, 63, 69, 83, 107, 127 Aleksei Diuzhov/123RF; 2, 3, 14 Sergio Magaña; 21 Lukiyanova Natalia frenta/Shutterstock

Printed in the United States of America

This book is to honor the cyclical and precise dream of the universe, the dream of the Earth, which keeps evolving in a silent, beautiful way, the people who knew how to read what was written in the stars, those who risked their lives to keep the message alive, those who had courage to reveal it, and all those who are living through these times.

CONTENTS

LIST OF EXERCISES

PREFACE

In 2011 I published a book in Italian, which came out in English and Spanish the following year: *2012–2021: The Dawn of the Sixth Sun*. In this book, the Toltec and Aztec wisdom tradition of central Mexico regarding time and the current transition from one cycle to another was revealed for the very first time. The book was greeted with skepticism, even disbelief, because it gave dates and cycles that differed in many respects from the widely known Mayan calendar. To this day they are being ignored, even though time has proven the Mayan calendar to have been badly misinterpreted, particularly with regard to the year 2012.

At the end of 2012, many people felt somehow disappointed because neither a global catastrophe nor the spiritual rebirth of humanity had taken place on December 21st. But in the teachings I received from the custodians of the Aztec and Toltec tradition, the transition from one time cycle to another wasn't tied to a particular date, but was more of an organic process. Nature herself illustrates this process every day: at dawn, darkness prevails, then little by little light starts breaking through until night turns to day. According to Toltec and Aztec wisdom, one time cycle gives way to another in exactly the same way.

These time cycles are known as "Suns." Each lasts, or "reigns," for 6,625 years, with 29 years being shared with the previous Sun and the following Sun during each transition. The Suns have individual features, but can be categorized into two groups—day, or light; and night, or dark—which alternate, just as day and night do.

Metaphorically speaking, this refers to the fact that during the day, when we are awake, our physical eyes are open and we are looking outward into the light. Looking outward is one of the main features of the Fifth Sun, the day Sun that is about to finish. During it, we have looked outward to find God, healing, and satisfaction. There has been a need to conquer territories, to be seen to succeed. We have sought happiness through the acquisition of external things, or through achievements in the outer world. For this reason, this kind of Sun is favorable for organized religions, war, finding happiness through others, our surroundings, travel, exploration, and so on, as history has confirmed over the last few thousand years.

On the other hand, when we close our eyes, we can only look inside, into darkness, into our unconscious, which is known in the Toltec tradition as our underworlds, the places where our dreams create our experience in the waking world. There we see the forces that we are unable to see in daylight, but which rule everything that exists. Therefore, dark or night Suns, such as the Sixth Sun that we are about to enter, are more spiritual Suns, where satisfaction comes from getting to know our inner self as well as from creating our own reality from the inside.

The beginning of the shift from one Sun to another is always marked by an eclipse. The beginning of this shift was marked by the full solar eclipse that was seen on July 11th, 1991, in Mexico City.

According to the Aztec and Toltec count, during the first 20 and half years of this transition we would witness external developments leading to the establishment of a different reality, and it is undeniable that the technological breakthroughs we have experienced during these years have led to the development of a "virtual reality" undreamed of back then. Moreover, people have used the new technology to seek spiritual answers far beyond those offered by the established patriarchal religions, and spiritual knowledge and practices have spread throughout the world. The speed with which this has happened and the fast-forward movement in communication and in our lives in general are also clear features of the dream world, in which, once we are lucid, that is, aware that we are dreaming, we can manifest anything immediately. So it can be said that we have already started preparing for the night Sun, although the day Sun is still influencing us. According to the Toltec count, December 21st, 2012, was the point at which the Suns would be exerting their influence equally on the collective mind.

The last nine years of the transition would then bring a real inner change, according to the prophecies, because everything that had been hidden would come to light. We can see this starting to happen now, with revelations about politics, religion, and pedophilia. Furthermore, humanity would then be facing its underworlds, its collective unconscious, and all the unresolved issues stored there, particularly in the years 2020 and 2021, which would be the most challenging ones, due to the influences that I will explain in this book.

I must confess that when I first wrote about this, I did so with absolute confidence in my teachers, but without really understanding how these changes would take place. Now, I realize that my faith was justified. Through their oral tradition, the Toltec and Aztec cultures maintained the correct interpretation of the cycles of time. The events of the last few years, and especially the crisis that we are facing today, are evidence of that.

Among the teachings I received was that day Suns tend to be patriarchal: masculine forces are in control and often repressing feminine forces, so the energies are imbalanced. One of the ways in which this manifests is through an imbalance in one of the most important feminine forces, Mother Earth, in the form of viruses and bacteria.

But the most important point I made then, which I will reiterate here, is that during this transition time, we should not be deceived by illusion or fall into the trap of fear and collective suffering. We are not powerless. It is how we perform our inner work that will determine how we come through this transition.

Therefore, as well as outlining the cosmic mathematics, I would like to present the inner techniques that reconnect us with two important energies of the Earth: *tlazolteotl*, which carries away everything that has outlived its usefulness, and *tlazohteotl*, which brings new skills and qualities. This will also lead to an understanding of the postures of Egyptian statues, for instance those of the goddess Sekhmet, and also Mexican statues, since all these teachings were hidden there in plain sight. We will also examine how to let the Earth take away everything that isn't useful to us anymore and provide us with the energy needed to create a new life, including a new, improved immune system.

Over the last few years I have been sharing teachings about spiritual awakening, lucid dreaming, and dying an enlightened death, but today I understand that the same ancient knowledge can be used to help us stay healthy and move into a new way of being, a new cycle. That's why the last Aztec spokesman, or *tlahtoani*, the young Cuauhtémoc, gave one final command a day before giving the Mexicans' power to the Spaniards: "Hide our treasure. Pass it from mothers to daughters, fathers to sons, teachers to students. Keep it safe, because it will be needed with the coming of the Sixth Sun." What he meant by "treasure" was not gold, as it was thought at the time, but knowledge.

The ancient people of Mexico knew of tiny particles of matter, from atoms to viruses to bacteria, and called them *michtons*. According to ancient tradition, there are four different types of Fire, and our immune system works with one of these, the Young Fire, to fight viruses and bacteria. This is a masculine type of Fire. However, we also need another type, the Female Fire, which is in charge of tackling what is about to come. In this book I will explain how to use both these Fires to create a strong immune system.

I will also talk about how to activate the Fire of knowledge, the Ancient Fire, known as *huehueteotl* in our tradition, to illuminate the dark times we are living in. This type of Fire enables us to have lucid dreams and to benefit from them, because in our dreams we create our waking experiences. For example, pandemics are normally related to violent dreams. In the collective mind of humanity, these dreams were instrumental in creating the coronavirus pandemic, as well as many of our environmental problems.

As individuals, we must all play our part in the transition to the Sixth Sun. In this book, I will teach you to lessen the violence in your dreams as well as provide other ways forward and other teachings from central Mexico. I will reveal the Toltec prophecies that time has proven to be true. To be real.

INTRODUCTION

In July 2005, a very intriguing person came on a course I was giving in Mexico City on the energy of the Pleiades. I remember that as I was teaching, he kept interrupting me, adding information about why the Pleiades were so important to the ancient Mexicans. Finally, another student became so annoyed by his constant interruptions that he exclaimed, "I didn't pay to listen to this man, but to you, so I'm going to ask him to keep quiet!"

During the lunch break the man approached me and I apologized for the other student's impatience, but added that he had interrupted me a lot.

He replied, "Look, I haven't come to learn from you, but to teach you about my lineage, to give you the knowledge that my teacher, Esteban, gave me. I've come to teach you about the times we are in now and the times to come."

During the course of my journey into the spiritual world I had met a lot of people who had boasted about having great revelations about the times to come, including the Second Coming of Christ and the return of Quetzalcóatl, so I didn't pay too much attention to him and told him that we could talk about it another time.

However, the following month, he came back to take another course. I recognized him immediately because once again he constantly interrupted me and annoyed the other students. I had to keep asking them to be patient with him, just to keep the peace.

Once again, during the lunch break he approached me and said, "I haven't come here to learn from you, but to teach you." This time, he added, "Because you are going to be the custodian of my lineage's message."

Obviously he was persistent, and by now I was slightly intrigued. So I said, "Alright. Let's have lunch together tomorrow. Then you can fill me in on your lineage's message."

The next day, over lunch, he talked about the four movements, *nahui ollin*, the foundation of the mathematics of the ancient Náhuatl cultures of Mexico, which include the Teotihuacan, the Toltec, and the Aztec. The four movements are based on the fact that each natural cycle is made up of four main steps, or movements. For example, a day is made up of the four main moments of dawn, midday, sunset, and midnight. Then there are the four moon phases—new, waxing, full, and waning—and of course there are the two solstices and two equinoxes that form the annual cycle as the Earth spins around the sun.

This was an interesting way of looking at cycles, but the teachings that had the greatest impact on me were the ones about the Long Count of central Mexico, the Toltec and Aztec count, which differed by nine years from the well-known Mayan Long Count and which talked about the end of the cycle nurturing human catastrophobia as well as a new humanity.

I was stunned by these predictions, because they were different from anything I had heard before. I had to admit that he was right: he had come to teach me. In fact, Hugo García, whom I now know as Hugo Nahui, was my first genuine teacher in the ancient Mexican tradition. Most of this book is based on his very first lesson that lunchtime in August 2005.

"After the July 2010 eclipse," he said, "the real Toltec wisdom will go out into the world, and you will be the one of its first spokespeople. Your work will start in Italy, then you will go to the UK, and then to the rest of the world."

This prophecy was fulfilled, since I wrote my first book in 2010 and it was published by an Italian publishing house in 2011, but sadly had little impact, as everybody was looking forward to either the end of the world or the birth of a new humanity on December 21st, 2012. As we know, neither of these prophecies came true, but Hugo's did, as my most recent books have been published by Hay House UK. So it was true—Italy and the UK—and since then I have been witnessing everything Hugo taught me, both in that first class and subsequent ones, coming to pass exactly as foretold by the Toltecs, including that during the years 2012 to 2021 humanity would go through its underworlds, which meant facing its unresolved problems.

I'm writing these lines in 2020, a year that has been practically catastrophic for humanity. I believe this is the first time in my entire life that I've said, "I'm sorry that I was right, that I had the right count." I'm living under the same restrictions as everyone else in these "unprecedented" times. Humanity has come to a crossroads: the dawn of the Sixth Sun. So, I will give you the Toltec prophecies for this Sun—both for the years 2021 to 2026 and for the thousands of years afterward. I will also give you a message of hope, a message that has been orally transmitted for hundreds of years, about how to live through this critical but wonderful period with grace.

Chapter 1

THE LONG COUNT

Hugo Nahui's first teachings were about the Aztec calendar. It was called that because the well-known Sun stone depicting it was carved during the Aztec era, but it is actually a compilation of the wisdom of many cultures—the Teotihuacan, the Toltec, and finally the Aztec. Hugo told me that the real name of the calendar was Cuauhxicalli, the house of the eagle, or *nahui ollin*, four movements.

As I mentioned earlier, the four movements correspond to the Náhuatl cultures' observations that there was a constant in the universe that was expressed not only through the cycles of the days, months, and years, but also through the larger cycles of the universe: the number four, repeating over and over on every scale, from the smallest moment to the longest era, making our universe cyclical and predictable.

These four movements are represented in the center of the calendar by a sun, which many people mistakenly think is sticking its tongue out, but actually the "tongue" is a *pedernal*, a flintstone knife of justice, which represents the Fifth Sun. The four squares surrounding it represent the four previous Suns, or the four movements of the day, the moon, and the year.

The four movements of the Aztec calendar

This calendar showing the great measures of time and space was branded as diabolic by the Spanish monk Fray Bernardino de Sahagún when the Spaniards arrived in Mexico. However,

I'm convinced it was actually this monk who compiled all the calendar's wisdom, especially the count of the days, and we owe him a great deal, especially now, as I realize more than ever that it is the calendar's presentation of repeated cycles based on the matrix of four that makes it the most outstanding prophetic instrument of the ancient world.

In a 20-day period, for example, every four days, one of the directions (east, north, west, and south) governs the calendar, and in this way it represents an endless number of different movements, such as the Quincunce, which represents the math of Venus and the moon, the rulers of the dream world.

The Quincunce

I will say more about that world later on, but to return to the Long Count, on the calendar it is shown by the two serpents with human faces that are on the outer ring. These serpents remind us of the huge effort the ancient Mexicans made to acquire precious knowledge, conquer their shadow and themselves, and awaken spiritually. This is really significant, since the outer ring represents all the people who will eventually awaken in a day, a lunar cycle, a year, or even 26,500 years. However long it takes, we will always acquire precious solar knowledge at the end of our learning cycle.

Coming back to the Long Count, I also learned in that first lesson that the two serpents represented a cycle that had already been seen before by many cultures and that it lasted 26,500 years. It was first observed by the Egyptians, who named it the precession of the equinoxes. The second place where this count was observed and calculated was in the ancient Mesopotamian civilization of Sumer, where it was divided into cycles of 2,160 years, which we now know as zodiacal ages. One of these cycles, which has been much discussed in modern times and finished some years ago, is the Age of Pisces. This was famous for the control exercised by three patriarchal religions: Judaism, Christianism, and Islam. This is now giving way to the more exploratory mentality of the Age of Aquarius, which is open to occultism, metaphysics, and new schools of thought.

Finally, another place where the Long Count was calculated, and even became the strongest influence on the collective consciousness, was in the Mayan and Toltec cultures, whose foundation was the number four, the matrix of the universe. Therefore, the ancient Toltecs and Aztecs divided the precession of the equinoxes into cycles of four, which they called Suns.

One of the things that got my attention during that first lesson was when my teacher said, "Have you seen what's being written about the end of the world and/or the golden race arriving in the year 2012? It's all based on a single statement from the oral tradition: 'On a *nahui ollin* day—that is, a four movements day—the Fifth Sun will finish its cycle with earthquakes, there will be a lot of suffering, and many people will pass away.'"

But according to the Toltec Mexihca calendar, December 21st, 2012, wasn't a four movements day, but a three serpents day. Furthermore, I believe the statement from the oral tradition cannot be taken literally. Of course, an earthquake is a tectonic plate movement, but it can also be the collapse of established social, economic, and political structures. When this happens, there is always a lot of suffering, because of people's laziness, resistance to change, and lack of discipline, and so it can be said that at the end of the Fifth Sun many will pass away, because the whole world will be forced to change.

I believe that if we look at the world today, we can see that this interpretation is more and more likely to be correct.

But before I start examining the Toltec prophecies and relating them to the events we are experiencing today, I would like to talk about the knowledge left by the Toltecs and Mexihcas with respect to the previous Sun, which is still affecting us. If we want to start addressing our current situation, this must be our starting point.

OUR INHERITANCE

The Toltec Mexihca culture only describes what happened during the last five Suns, or 33,625 years. I know that the Mayan and the Vedic traditions go back further, but the main issue for us now is dealing with the legacy of these times. The relatively new science of epigenetics is showing that we inherit the effects of all the traumas our ancestors have lived through. Just as we can analyze our own family history in order to carry out a personal healing process, so we can look at our great human family history in order to find out what we have inherited and how we can heal on a collective level.

At first glance, the Toltec tales of previous Suns seem preposterous. However, once we get familiar with the Toltecs' way of thinking, we start to understand that they were using metaphors to describe historical events.

The very first thing we need to understand is that the Suns, the periods of 6,625 years, were compared to specific moments in a day. We need to consider this when using this ancient tradition prophetically. But first, let's go back to the First Sun.

The First Sun: The Sun of the Jaguar

The First Sun metaphorically reigned from sunset to midnight, which was why it is regarded as a Sun of darkness. There is said to have been no movement then; it was a period of great stability. Ancient traditions worldwide, including the Chichimec and the Otomí of ancient Mexico, stated that there were huge beings on Earth at that time, giants who were much taller than average humans and who spread around the world. Other cultures reported that gods walked the Earth.

According to the Toltec tradition, the huge beings were dishonest which why they became extinct. So, the people of the First Sun left us the idea that human decay began with a lack of honesty, a burden we have been carrying ever since.

The Second Sun: The Sun of Wind

The Second Sun reigned from midnight to dawn, just as the Sixth Sun will, so the Sixth Sun will have some of the features of the Second. That's why we need to be especially aware of what we have inherited from this period.

During the Second Sun it is said that humanity turned into apes or monkeys. Many people are confused by this, because they believe the ancient Mexicans were talking about prehistory, but according to Darwin's theory of evolution, wasn't it the other way around?

In the ancient Toltec tradition, however, the ape or monkey is the archetype that symbolizes pleasure, dance, and sex, and is associated with creativity. Therefore, this Sun was, at least at the beginning, at midnight, a time of relative happiness, creativity, and pleasure. Midnight, however, is a time of manifesting dreams without any moral framework, and the people in that Sun decided to manifest pleasure and power instead of evolution. Under the cover of darkness, they lost their discernment and found themselves succumbing not only to lust, but to all forms of excess. It was then that humanity lost strength of will, discipline, and purpose. We can see that something similar is narrated in the biblical story of Sodom and Gomorrah.

At the end of this period, it is said that the Wind came and blew everything away. The Wind symbolizes old energy, particularly the Black Wind of the North, which is equivalent to karma. Therefore, we need to understand that the legacy of the Second Sun will be significant in our time. Its great trap is refusing to change until everything is blown away, and this explains why there are so many people nowadays who can't overcome their fear of change and would rather cling to an unworkable system or sit in front of their TV set until things are back to the way they were before. On the other hand, others have already started to change the way they live.

The Third Sun: The Sun of Fire

The Third Sun's legacy is one of our most profound lessons. Metaphorically speaking, this Sun reigned from dawn to midday, the two moments of the day when the sun is the main force and provides more masculine qualities.

And here comes the shocker! According to tradition, during the Third Sun humanity became *guajolotes*—turkeys! Of course, this is another metaphor. The turkey symbolizes the ego. This can be seen in the bird itself: aesthetically, turkeys are not the most attractive creatures in the animal kingdom, but in their mating ritual, they puff themselves up, convinced that they look ravishing! In fact, the verb "to strut," *pavonearse* in Spanish, comes from the turkey's mating dance.

Thus, the turkey represents the illusion of feeling superior to others, the illusion in which the best-looking, wealthiest, and most successful people are usually trapped. Conversely, it can also represent the illusion of feeling inferior to others, the prison in which most of us have been confined by society, especially the media, holding up models of beauty and success for us to emulate. If we reflect for a moment, we can see the legacy of the Third Sun in the way that many people worship celebrities or royalty. But, as one of my greatest teachers would say, "These are only illusions from the reflection in the mirror."

It is said that at the end of the Third Sun, a rain of raging Fire wiped almost everything out, and turkeys were the only ones left. The burnt appearance of their faces warns us that false ego can be as destructive as a raging Fire.

It is believed that this rain of Fire could have been caused by volcanic eruptions in the Pacific Ring of Fire, or perhaps by a nuclear war between advanced civilizations. We cannot know for certain, but we can heed the turkeys' warning.

In the ancient cultures of Mexico, initiated warriors, priests, and governors would be given a small turkey made of jade after they had completed their training and had overcome the illusion of the reflection in the mirror. This was so that they would remember that they could never be less but equally could never be more than the rest of humanity.

The Fourth Sun: The Sun of Water

The Fourth Sun reigned from midday to sunset, so was considered a day sun, one of masculine dominance, although sunset is a much more feminine force and a time when everything that affects the collective consciousness happens during the unconscious state. It was said that during this Sun, the Earth was flooded and humans became marine creatures.

We can explain this flooding in two different ways. The first is that it was the well-known Great Flood described in the Bible and many ancient legends. According to our tradition, if that were the case, the Great Flood would have happened between *c.*13,000 and 10,000 years ago.

Of course, the flood may not have been literal, but metaphorical. In the Toltec tradition, the element of Water represents emotions and change. Therefore, we can see that these would have been years of sudden, unexpected, and often inexplicable change. We are experiencing this again now as part of the legacy of this Sun.

According to the tradition, there are actually four different types of Water:

Water (rain) that does not fall: drought

This type of Water represents everything we lack. All of us have, or have had, areas of terrible drought in our lives—in our emotions, work, finances, and so on. Our planet is a reflection of our collective inner selves and the massive Fires that have occurred in the last few years have been reflecting the great inner drought that we are suffering as individuals.

Water that falls as hail and destroys

The ancients described this type of Water as hail because it destroyed blooming, i.e. self-expression and fulfillment. On a personal level, it represents addictions, diseases, bad relationships, and all the situations in which we are self-destructive.

As our planet is a loyal reflection of ourselves, the rough weather, hurricanes, and typhoons that we see nowadays show us how much inner, individual hail is falling. The time has come for us to take responsibility for our own Water in order to help our beloved Earth.

Water that falls suddenly and causes floods

Floods are excess Water, so of course this third type of Water refers to all the excesses that we have in our lives. Work, guilt, painful emotions, food, materialism... I believe the excessive consumerism of affluent society has left us completely flooded by this type of Water, since some people are very poor (droughts), whereas others are extremely rich (floods), resulting in a level of inequality that has never been seen before in human history.

Water that makes it possible for all things to grow in harmony

This fourth type of Water is the gentle rain that helps everything in the natural world to grow. There are many spiritual practices to heal our inner Water and turn it into the rain that will help us to grow and to live in the mental paradise where we are balanced in our own Water.

Now, having the whole picture, we can see how the story of everything being flooded is one of an increase in destructive emotions and the response to them resulting in an excess of emotion. Some of the biggest burdens that we have collectively been carrying were generated during this period: an addiction to suffering; a tendency to bring trouble on ourselves; the inequality and disease that make our lives miserable.

It is easy to see that we need to eradicate this legacy of the Fourth Sun—the ideas that we are here to suffer, that we must just put up with things, and that the rich will never get to heaven. The Earth is a wonderful place that can be a paradise or a crucifixion—it is totally up to us.

The Fifth Sun: The Sun of the Flintstone Knife

So, we have reached modern times, the Fifth Sun, the era that will end next year, 2021. Here we are as a human species, sharing the inheritance of the Suns that have gone before and ignoring the heavy burden we are all carrying as a result of incarnating on this planet at this time.

The Fifth Sun is represented by the well-known image of the sun with the flintstone-knife tongue seen on the Aztec calendar. Unfortunately, every time that people around the world see this representation of the Aztec calendar, they mistake it for the Mayan calendar. To make things worse, if you do an Internet search for "Mayan calendar," the first image that appears on more than half of the sites is that of the Aztec calendar.

I would like to clarify that we are talking about two different calendars here. Both are based on the numbers 13 and 20, but their Long Counts differ.

The Fifth Sun

According to the Long Count of central Mexico, the Fifth Sun, also known as the Flintstone Knife Sun, dates back approximately 6,600 years. All our official history has taken place during this Sun. Unfortunately, as a species, we only have any real regard for the history of the West, minimizing that of the East, and neglecting and even destroying that of the Americas.

The Fifth Sun has lasted from sunset to midnight, which means it started during the masculine vibration of the day and should have taken on a more feminine or at least more balanced energy around 6,000 years ago. However, those of us who are familiar with this count know that something unusual happened then.

Around that time, there was a ritual of cutting the head off a statue of the Sumerian sun goddess, which led to the rise of an unimaginably patriarchal culture. This contradicted everything that should have happened, according to the Long Count. We may conclude that there was a group of people who refused to accept the rule of the feminine night and moon and so brought about a highly controlling masculine and solar hegemony by means of the dark arts.

However it came about, this unnatural order led to the suppression of women, minorities, and particular races, and the creation of patriarchal religions. Nowadays, many people believe this is the way things should be, and, worst of all, it is the only reality that exists on almost the entire planet. We are living in a Sun of injustice, a time when small groups exploit others, when racial inequality prevails, causing endless pain and suffering, and when all sorts of atrocities are justified in the name of religion, or the name of a vengeful god who favors only one religion or race.

So, this is a Sun whose legacy is one of inequality, suffering, and wrath. That's why some cultures have called it the Sun of Rage.

◈◈◈

Back to my first lesson with Hugo… The first thing I learned was that we would be experiencing the transition from the Fifth to the Sixth Sun and that it had already started. What Hugo told me then is still fresh in my memory:

"In the central Mexican count, the change will be gradual, just as in nature, when dawn slowly pierces the veil of darkness, giving rise to a new day. The veil is the time between 1991 and 2021, when the reign of the Sixth Sun will start."

He added, "This shift started with the solar eclipse of July 11th, 1991, which was seen in Hawaii, Mexico City, and parts of South America. That was when the Sixth Sun started taking over, little by little, from the Fifth Sun."

He said that the Suns would exert the same amount of influence over the collective consciousness on December 21st, 2012. After that midpoint, the Fifth Sun would gradually start losing power until a lunar eclipse on May 26th, 2021, would mark its setting. However, the collapse of the old system would still be impacting us until the ceremony of the New Fire—a ceremony held by the peoples of central Mexico, including Toltecs and Aztecs—on November 24th, 2026, which would mark the birth of a new stage in the collective consciousness of humanity.

He mentioned that the last nine years of the transition would be the most complicated for us, since we would have to go through our underworlds.

This was the very first time that I had heard about the Long Count, planetary alignments that went far beyond astrology, New Fires, etc. Many of you may be in the same position now. So, in the next chapter I will relate part of my research into what Hugo told me, and then we will be able to see the extent to which the Toltec prophecies have come true. After that, we will look at the years to come. Then, finally, I will offer solutions and practical exercises so that we can live through these times in the best way for us all.

Chapter 2

THE PATH THROUGH
THE UNDERWORLDS

That afternoon in 2005, I was fascinated by the Toltec teachings and needed to find out more. I started having weekly lessons with Hugo, but I also undertook further research on my own. First of all, I researched the Long Counts.

THE LONG COUNTS

When I started my research, all the information that was available about Long Counts focused on one date: December 21st, 2012. I couldn't find any mention of 2021 at all. However, I found that eclipses were considered omens of misfortune by many ancient civilizations. Also, soon after meeting Xolotl, my other teacher in Mexican tradition, and learning from him how to read the ancient Mexican pictographs, I learned that the symbol for a lunar eclipse was a crocodile, representing Mother Earth, eating a circle with a cross in the center, representing the moon.

Guided by this information, I visited Xochicalco, an archeological site in Morelos, whose principal jewel is the Temple of Quezalcóatl. This monument to the precious knowledge of the Xochicalca culture, which is officially considered post-Teotihuacan, post-Mayan, and pre-Toltec, contains a stone carving of a gathering of wise men, who, by their ethnic characteristics, were clearly Maya, Olmec, Mixtec, Zapotec, and Xochicalca meeting to adjust the calendar.

The most interesting thing I found was that the symbol of the crocodile devouring the moon appeared on the walls, which made it clear to me that the most important factors, or some of the most important, at the beginning and end of the count were lunar eclipses.

Also, since the Toltec and Aztec splendor occurred after all the previously mentioned cultures, there must have been further deliberations where the Long Count was validated and the calendar adjusted if necessary. Thus, the Long Count of central Mexico must have followed the Mayan one from the south of Mexico, and been refined along the way, and therefore it seemed probable that this count was the more accurate one.

Carvings at the Temple of Quetzalcóatl, Xochicalco

*Symbol of the crocodile devouring the moon
at the Temple of Quetzalcóatl, Xochicalco*

I continued my training with Hugo and Xolotl, learning about lucid dreaming and the Mexican identity, which became my main interests, but at the same time I was observing how Hugo's personal predictions were coming true and how the great prophecy of the Long Count was being fulfilled as well. Now, I have no doubt the Long Count of central Mexico is the right one.

THE TRANSITION

The Toltec count aligns perfectly with the prophecy that Hugo told me about:

> *The change will begin with*
> *the eclipse of July 11th, 1991.*

That eclipse was advertised widely on television, on radio, and in the print media, along with a warning not to look at it directly, for fear of going blind. I was very young, but I remember watching it with my family through the skylight at home and experiencing the shadow that fell over us for that minute in the middle of the day.

> *The first 20 years or so will see external*
> *changes for the most part, but internal changes*
> *will gradually become apparent.*

If we consider everything that the Sixth Sun has brought, the accuracy of this prophecy is undeniable. The year after the eclipse, bandwidth expansion brought the possibility of accessing the Internet from personal computers. This eventually led to cell phones—devices that today are more important to the majority of the population than their partners and friends, something that was unthinkable back in 1991.

Photoshop, the software program that allows us to edit photographs and enhance images, had also just been developed then. And so a large number of people began to be alienated from themselves through seeking to look like supermodels or profiles made by technology and almost impossible for humans to imitate. A variety of eating and personality disorders followed.

GPS also arrived, first as specialist technology used by the military to find and track people, then as a way for us to pinpoint our location in our cars and on our cell phones and find our way to our destination without the need to see physical signs, read a physical map, or ask anyone for directions.

Little by little, direct communication with the external world was reduced. As the years passed, emails and text messages arrived, replacing human contact, direct speech, letters, and phone calls. Imperceptibly, technology began to generate an inner lockdown, a voluntary one, where we remained within ourselves. As I wrote this book, we had an outer lockdown that was mandatory.

Then, of course, Facebook arrived, the most important social network of the Sixth Sun so far. We no longer had to make a physical effort to get to know someone; with the photos on our computer or phone, we could form new friendships and gather families and strangers together—all without human contact, hugs, or fights.

I now understand why it was said that the Fifth Sun was a time of looking outside for everything—things, people, satisfaction, God—but the Sixth Sun would be a time to look inside, to what would seem like a dream world. Of course the change could not happen immediately, and in fact it has been gradual. But little by little, we have stopped looking at the exterior world directly and started seeing it via a computer or phone.

We can also observe how in those years Buddhism expanded in the East, and meditation, yoga, astrology, and other spiritual subjects and practices began to be more widely known in the West. As the prophecy said, "Internal changes will gradually become apparent."

In the last part of this first phase of change, leading up to our planetary alignment with the center of the galaxy on December 21st, 2012, we entered an era of automation in which human workers began to be replaced by machines, completely changing the global economy.

On December 21st, 2012, as mentioned earlier, the Fifth and Sixth Suns were equally influential. Astronomically, there was an alignment of several planets in the constellation of Taurus, where the Pleiades and the center of the galaxy are located. I want to clarify here that in the ancient tradition, alignments and eclipses are seen from a geocentric viewpoint. It is when seen from Earth that the planets appear to be in line; it is not really that they are aligned in the universe.

NEW POSSIBILITIES OR REPEAT PATTERNS?

In my later classes with Hugo and Xolotl, I learned about the importance of the Pleiades to the ancient Mexicans. I mentioned earlier that the Long Count in the Aztec calendar was portrayed as two snakes with human faces and feathers. If we look at them carefully, we can see that in the feathers they both have seven little circles and one bigger one that might be serving as an earring for both human heads. It was through this that I learned that those seven circles represented the Pleiades and the earring corresponded to our sun, and that the Long Count was based on the orbit of our sun around the Pleiades.

In Náhuatl, the ancient Toltec and Aztec language, this orbit is called Tianquiztli. It is said that proof of this can be seen in the fact that Templo Mayor in Mexico City was dedicated to the sun and the identical Templo Mayor of Tlatelolco, an area of Mexico City where the main allies of the Mexihca lived, was dedicated to the Pleiades. The market was located there, so we Mexicans still call it *tianguis*, the bazaar, in memory of Tianquiztli, the orbit of our Earth around the Pleiades and hence the cosmic order.

Despite not being visible to the naked eye, the Pleiades were particularly important to many ancient cultures, such as the Celts, Greeks, Mexicans, and Hawaiians.

The sun takes 26,500 years to orbit the Pleiades, which gives us more information about the nature of the Suns and the cosmic cycles. We are now reaching the same position in relation to the Pleiades that we were in during the transition from the First Sun to the Second. We must revise the lessons and legacies of these Suns, so we don't repeat our mistakes. But the Pleiades are now in a radically different position in the universe than they were then, which makes it possible for us to change our destiny in this new Sun by combining the energy of the repeat position with that of the new one to gain a better outcome.

The great lesson of the First Sun was that lack of honesty brought ruin. So, this is a good time to ask ourselves: "Am

I being honest? Am I being honest with myself, about my feelings, about my beliefs, and in what I say? Or is the collective speaking through me? Am I just parroting what I've been told my entire life?"

As we move into the Sixth Sun, we need to be honest with ourselves. Take a moment to reflect on these questions:

❀ Who do I believe I am?

❀ Who am I?

❀ How would I like to spend this transition?

❀ Am I willing to change and enter a different world without missing the previous one?

Next, we should evaluate our governments and mainstream media. Can they be trusted? Are they telling us the truth? Are they pushing an agenda, and if so, what and why? We should draw our own conclusions and consider whether we are creating something new or simply repeating patterns ingrained in our unconscious for the last 26,500 years.

In the Second Sun, the weaknesses that ultimately wiped people out were fear of change, laziness, and lack of discipline. I believe that with these very things are the Achilles heel of humanity today. How are you facing the current crisis? Are you afraid of what will happen? Are you paralyzed, just hoping that normal life will be restored? It's not very likely now. Are you making the changes you need to look after yourself, be at peace with yourself, and adapt to the new phase? Or are you too lazy? Believe me, if you are sitting in front of the television or your phone, just waiting for things to get back to normal, you are under the influence of the Second Sun, and what happened then was that the Wind arrived and swept everything away. The Wind is old energy—karma, if you want to see it that way—and it will do the same this time around, so those who don't want to change will be forced to or perish.

But all is not lost: if we learn the lessons of the First and Second Suns as we transition from the Fifth to the Sixth, new possibilities will open up for us.

The Sixth Sun is called Iztac Tonatiuh, or "the White Sun." "White" refers to the prophecy of the return of Quetzalcóatl, the essence of God or white energy, or Quequetzalcóatl, plural, meaning "those in whom the serpent rises," the serpent being the Mexican equivalent of the kundalini of Eastern traditions. So, the Quequetzalcóatl are those who have acquired precious knowledge and spiritual enlightenment. In other traditions, such people are known as avatars, or those with Christ Consciousness, or Buddha nature.

So this prophecy is telling us that it is worth the effort to overcome the obstacles of these times, adapt to the new order, and seek spiritual knowledge. We may even think that it refers to us personally and that we can reach enlightenment in the new Sun. I like to think this way and am working to make this my future. Part of this is seeking to understand the nature of the new world we are moving into and the most graceful ways of reaching it, which we will address in the following chapters.

But first, let us return to Hugo's prophecy at the end of my first lesson with him: that from 2012 to 2021, humanity would pass through its underworlds.

THE UNDERWORLDS

First, let us clarify the concept of underworlds. The orthodox view is that "the underworld" is where the ancients believed we would go after death. Indeed, we will go there after death, but this is a very limited truth. Just as sophisticated ancient cultures as the Egyptians, Mayans, and Toltecs, among others, believed that the sun died every evening to be reborn the following day, so "the underworld" was a metaphorical way of describing one of the places we go at night when we sleep. As our dreams create a large part of our waking experience, our underworlds are in fact places of creation. They are the places where we are forced to re-create ourselves, as they are the places where we face all our unresolved problems, our unconscious negative patterns, our inertia and self-destructiveness, our negative ancestral legacy, and our "old Winds," our karma.

In the Toltec Mexihca tradition, there are nine of these underworlds. They are all described metaphorically. They exist on a collective as well as a personal level. We all make a personal contribution to the collective underworlds. Consequently, we cannot avoid responsibility for any of them. What we can do is analyze how we have contributed to them. Then we can accept our responsibility and make changes accordingly.

We are going through our underworlds on a collective level during this time of transition at a rate of one year per underworld, but the previous underworlds are continuing to have an influence on us as well.

2013: The First Underworld

This is described as the underworld where we cross from one river to another. This refers to crossing from the waking state to the dream state and from life to death.

As I mentioned earlier, the Sixth Sun has seen cell phones develop from luxury objects into essential ones. The process whereby technology, video games, and social networking are turning our attention from the external world hasn't ended yet, and one way or another we will be forced to cross the river and look inside ourselves.

2014: The Second Underworld

This is a place where there are two mountains divided by a path. Every time we want to walk between the mountains, they move together, crushing us and sending us back to the beginning of the path.

This represents all the destructive patterns that we repeat time and time again, both as individuals and as a collective, despite the suffering the mountains, metaphorically speaking, cause us.

That suffering can be on a huge scale. Even two World Wars and the complete destruction of many civilizations have not been enough for us, collectively speaking. We always start over, seeing one another as strangers or enemies, in spite of our shared humanity. Although we have passed through this underworld, we are feeling its influence now, as nationalism is rising and we are even seeing race riots. Once again, it seems, the human species is repeating a destructive pattern and is about to be crushed by the two mountains.

What can we do? We can all act on a personal level by analyzing the destructive patterns we have been repeating in our own lives. The way to break free from this underworld is to acknowledge these patterns, then decide how we can achieve what we want without them, without laziness, and without a lack of discipline.

2015: The Third Underworld

This is a hill covered with obsidian knives, on which we cut ourselves every time we walk over them.

This is a very simple way of describing what we have inherited from the Fourth Sun: an addiction to suffering. Phrases such as "This world is a vale of tears," "We are here to suffer," and "It's easier for a camel to pass through the eye of a needle than for a rich man to enter the Kingdom of Heaven" illustrate this underworld perfectly.

It is an unfortunate human tendency to always have unresolved problems, whether they relate to health, relationships, emotions, and currently even infections. According to Hugo, this tendency comes from our memories of being a young baby who could only ask for food or get attention by crying. We continue this into later life, not necessarily by crying, but by seeking attention in negative, destructive ways. But the price we pay is a very high one, in the form of disease, poverty, lack, or bad relationships.

On a personal basis, it's very easy to identify the areas where we are addicted to suffering, for these are the areas we're constantly having trouble with. What is a constant problem for you: health, abundance, relationships, sexuality?

On a collective level, I still remember quite well the time of the Fifth Sun, when most people in a conventional marriage, following an organized religion, and earning a good wage believed they were happy, or were at least satisfied. However, under the increasing influence of the Sixth Sun, we are seeing more and more people experiencing personal crises, going through divorces, questioning their beliefs, and losing their faith, not to mention their job. Society is overrun with depression and anxiety, and the number of psychiatric patients has dramatically increased, leading to an increase in the prescription of anti-depressants and anti-psychotics. Even worse is the fact that the drugs aren't mitigating the addiction to pain we have developed as a species, only leading us, one by one, to the hill of knives, where we hurt ourselves more and more.

But, believe me, the end of this cycle is a great opportunity for us as a society to accept that this problem exists and that we need to bring all this suffering to an end. Not only do we need to observe what's happening, but also to resolve to change— on a collective level. We can do it. It's actually easier to take advantage of the current lockdown to make changes, initially on a personal level, than to cling to the outdated ideas and suffering of the previous Sun.

2016: The Fourth Underworld

This is described as a place of freezing Winds where we are all covered with a layer of ice that prevents us from moving. Of course, being frozen goes against the spiritual truth that movement and change are inevitable.

Ask yourself where you are frozen. Are there things that you have always wanted to achieve or create but haven't ever got round to starting? Admitting where you have been lazy or undisciplined will help you to get out of this trap of the First Sun and to see clearly your contribution to the layer of ice freezing humanity.

The influence of this underworld has become more evident now because it has combined with that of the second underworld. Being frozen into destructive patterns has led to the revival of outdated political views and movements. We can see this in the tendency to fight one another rather than accept the great universal truth that we are all one and should all move forward together. Sadly, things may get even worse before we thaw out enough to move in a different direction.

2017: The Fifth Underworld

The fifth underworld in the Aztec and Toltec mythology is a place where fierce Winds blow a flag incessantly. For the ancient people, strong Winds symbolized the influence of our ancestors. When they blew, we would face unresolved family issues or repeat negative family patterns, just as a flag flaps over and over in the Wind.

Lately, a new branch of science called epigenetics has revealed that the traumas of one generation are handed down to those following. If left unresolved, they can have unfortunate physical and emotional consequences.

To understand your contribution to this underworld, analyze the destructive patterns that have repeated in your family. You may see the traumas of your ancestors surfacing in your own life in the form of problems with relationships, health, or finances.

In 2020, we even re-experienced the pandemic past of humanity. Yet, most people live in this underworld without realizing its existence. This is "the invisible prison of the ancestors," a prison that the majority of prisoners don't know they are in.

There are people, of course, who have understood their family inheritance and decided to break its patterns, or curses, through effort and will. Now we need to do this on a collective level. It may seem that the fifth underworld is affecting all of humanity. But there is the possibility that the collective ancestral patterns of dominance and exploitation will be broken in the new Sun.

2018: The Sixth Underworld

In the Toltec tradition, this underworld is a place where wild beasts devour our heart, causing us eternal suffering. This is a very powerful metaphor for destructive emotions. If we are full of anger, sadness, or guilt, it makes perfect sense.

Reflect for a moment on the emotions that have been dominating you this year. What are they? Happiness, compassion, and love? Or anger, fear, and resentment? How have you contributed on a personal basis to the collective emotional destiny? If not quite as you would wish, don't blame yourself, but resolve to change, to dream a new dream, to make a new start.

2019: The Seventh Underworld

This is a place where we are hunted and wounded by arrows. However, if we avoid being wounded, we can escape from death.

What does this mean? The arrows represent our words. Therefore, in this underworld we are hunted and wounded by all the words that we have uttered that have been without wisdom. By "words," I am also referring to thoughts.

Before you contemplate your personal contribution to this collective underworld, I would like to ask you a question from the Mexican tradition that made a great impression on me: "What do you use when you speak or think, flowers or arrows?" Ask yourself about the effect of your words and thoughts on yourself and others. Do your words have the scent of flowers or a bellicose, wounding tone? Now you will be able to understand your personal contribution to this underworld.

On the collective level, the power of words and thoughts is more palpable every day, since more information is becoming available day by day, thanks to technology. This should help us to evolve; in other words, to bring flowers to our individual lives as well as to humanity. On the other hand, threats and cyberattacks have become more common, and the destructive power of social networks is becoming apparent. Furthermore, we need to consider the arrows that look like flowers but just undermine us, and even our faith in humanity.

Which will prevail, flowers or arrows? It is up to us to decide.

2020: The Eighth Underworld

In Toltec mythology, the eighth underworld is described as a pitch-black place, and when people or souls find themselves there, they don't know which way to go. It is an underworld of uncertainty. Nothing could better describe the world we are living in.

It is undeniable that humanity is currently engulfed in total uncertainty. There are still many people who are denying the obvious and refusing to see the changes that are coming. Others accept that there will be change, but are afraid of it. But there are those whose inner being is driving them forward to create a new way of living, one full of happiness and harmony, and a new way of supporting themselves that helps both people and planet.

Now, you should start analyzing how much you have been contributing to this underworld. You need to ask yourself: "How have I reacted to current events? Am I refusing to change or adapting with joy and acceptance?"

In addition, we should all take note of the political elections and international affairs of the next few years, because then it will become clear to us if, as a collective consciousness, we are still aligning with the Fifth Sun or opening up to the Sixth Sun.

Looking closely at the center of the Aztec calendar (*p.14*), we can see that although we don't know which way to go now, there will inevitably be a great change. We can see that the Fifth Sun, which represents movement, is located in the center of the calendar, together with the other squares that, as I mentioned before, can mean many different things, such as previous Suns. If we look even more closely, we can see, right in the middle of all the squares, a pair of eagle's talons. This means that the old must be destroyed before the arrival of the new. So, night will be destroyed by the coming day, and vice versa. The Fifth Sun, with its way of life, will be destroyed by the Sixth Sun, the Sixth Sun will be destroyed by the Seventh, and so forth. On and on it goes, in an eternal cycle of destruction and renewal. So, one thing we can be certain of is that there will be change.

2021: The Ninth Underworld

According to the ancient but at the same time contemporary Toltec cosmology, the last underworld is the one where we find peace, not only in death but also in rest. If we stop and think for a moment, we will realize that we are already under the influence of this underworld, due to the lockdown we are experiencing. Travel has stopped, economic activity has almost stopped, even personal and family relations have stopped.

In analyzing your personal relationship with this underworld, you just need to ask yourself, "Am I in peace with myself? Have I been able to accept what is going on?" If your answer is "No," you still have many lessons to learn before the arrival of the Sixth Sun.

Despite the fact that the Long Count will finish with the lunar eclipse of May 26th, 2021, the influence of this underworld will not end until the arrival of the New Fire on November 24th, 2026. Hence, we still have time to contribute positively to the collective underworlds, as we will discuss in later chapters.

〖◌◌◌◌◌◌◌◌◌◌◌◌◌◌◌◌〗

MY UNDERWORLDS

To finish this review of our path through the underworlds, take a pen and a piece of paper. Jot down and recap what has been discussed in this chapter, and once again ask yourself:

❋ How long do I spend every day on my phone, unaware of the inner world or the outer world?

❋ What destructive patterns am I repeating?

❋ How addicted am I to suffering?

❋ Am I afraid to change, or am I too lazy? Or could it be a lack of discipline that is preventing me from reaching my highest potential?

❋ Which negative family patterns am I repeating?

❋ Are my words beautiful or wounding?

❀ Do I know where I'm going? Am I leading the way?

❀ Am I at peace with myself?

When you have finished, you will be aware of the baggage that you are carrying, both personally and as part of the collective legacy of the previous Suns. This will be the material we will be working with later on in this book.

❦❦❦❦❦❦❦❦❦❦❦❦

Chapter 3

THE UNCERTAIN PRESENT

After seeing the accuracy of the Toltec Long Count, I knew I had to write a new book to make this information more widely available. So I contacted my publishers, and once they had given the go-ahead, the first thing I did was get in touch with Hugo Nahui. This was because a large part of the information I am presenting here came from his teaching and lineage.

How well I remember our conversation. It took place on April 26th, 2020. Having just taught my last class before all gatherings were limited by the Mexican government to 10 people maximum, I was on my way back to Playa del Carmen, in the southeast of Mexico, where I was living at the time. For the first time I realized the extent of the global transformation that was underway. The almost empty airport, the social distancing, the mandatory face coverings, and the excessive security measures upset me beyond measure. Filling out a long security questionnaire about my recent contacts and activities and, of course, having my temperature taken really brought home to me that we were facing a new order.

With most flights cancelled and all shops and cafés closed, I had extra time at the airport, so was happy to settle down and call my great teacher and friend Hugo. To my surprise, he was completely unperturbed, even happy about the global situation. Why?

A GLOBAL IMBALANCE

First of all, Hugo and I spoke of the lessons he had given me all those years ago and how accurate his predictions had been. I told him about the book I was writing and the research I had previously conducted. As I looked around me, unsettled by the strange new world I was in, he reminded me of the effect that unbalanced elements—Fire, Wind (Air), Water, and Earth—have on the Earth and on us:

✾ An imbalance of Fire in humans produces anger, inflammation, cancer, and abnormal growths.

❀ An imbalance of Wind produces respiratory problems, brings the consequences of actions on a personal and global level, and causes difficulties in manifesting anything in life.

❀ An imbalance of Water creates emotional problems, addictions, droughts (situations of lack), floods (excess of all kinds), and hail (destructive situations), on both a personal and global level.

❀ Finally, an imbalance of Earth—both our inner Earth and our Mother Earth—produces poverty, infections, and earthquakes.

I had learned all these things many years before. I had taught them on many of my own courses. Now I realized that they were preparation for understanding our current era and the extreme situation we were in. What else could the elements teach us?

In the ancient Toltec tradition there are four Fires, four Winds, four Earths, and four Waters. Both Fires and Winds have three male types and one female. With Waters and Earths, the opposite occurs. Therefore, these are the elements that are currently the most unbalanced.

Earth

Let us begin with Earth. A lack of balance here is first apparent through poverty, which has increased worldwide in recent decades, with the gap between rich and poor growing larger every day.

If the imbalance is not recognized and addressed during this early stage, as of course it has not been, it moves to a second level. This is when infections arise. We have had many examples, from AIDS and Ebola all the way to the coronavirus pandemic.

If we do not change the path we're on at this point, we will fall into a premature state of decay, with a massive number of deaths. Therefore, I sincerely hope this book, and others with similar messages, will lead us back to a healthy path and restore our relationship with the element of Earth.

Water

With Water, the principal component of our blood, an imbalance is first seen through emotional problems. As I mentioned earlier, these have intensified lately. It is also well known that the trafficking of illegal drugs has increased worldwide. Excessive use of psychotropic substances demonstrates that Water is, on a personal and global level, in a state of true imbalance.

On a planetary level, we also see this imbalance in the many droughts, which reflect a collective lack; floods, which reflect human excess; and hail or snowstorms, which represent destruction.

Fire

Fire is not as unbalanced as Earth and Water at present, but that's not to say that it is balanced. On a personal level, a Fire imbalance presents first as anger, which we can see is on the rise today. Then it manifests as inflammations of all kinds, all the way to the development of cancer, which is already one of the leading causes of death around the world.

On a global level, we have experienced a rise in devastating Fires in places such as Australia and California, while the lack of female Fire, one of the four types of Fire, has caused personal relationships to deteriorate. The Fire of wisdom is, however, increasing, as can be seen in the numbers of people who have spiritually awakened. In other people, though, it is being constantly extinguished. So, overall, a more divided society is being created.

Wind

Wind is also one of the less unbalanced elements at the moment, but this is changing. This is because of what is happening with the four different types of Wind: the Red Wind of the West, which purifies, is blowing with less strength; the Blue Wind of the South, which removes thorns from our path, is almost blocked; the Yellow Wind of the East, which brings good advice and fortune, is still being felt by a group of people; but the Black Wind of the North, the black Fire, which brings misfortune and disgrace, has unleashed its full strength during these times.

This imbalance in the elements is how we have reached 2020 and the underworld of complete darkness. I hope this explanation has shed some light on the situation.

Our current problems have come mainly from the imbalance of Earth. The first problem is poverty, which has been with us for so long it is considered a normal state of affairs. As we have not addressed this, we have moved to the second level, so we are facing infections such as the coronavirus pandemic, which will be followed by others. Meanwhile, poverty is spreading alarmingly quickly, with the loss of jobs worldwide. If we do not resolve these issues, we will reach the next level: premature societal decay, followed by massive deaths.

This process of escalation is in danger of happening not only with Earth, but with all of the elements. It closely resembles the story of the Four Horsemen of the Apocalypse (in which the figures symbolize the evils of conquest, war, famine and plague to come at the end of the world). As Hugo reminded me, in the Náhuatl tradition, every cycle is made up of four steps.

A TRANSFORMATION PROCESS IN FOUR STEPS

Back in the almost deserted airport on April 26th, after going through security I had another call with Hugo. During this conversation I commented on the accuracy of the Toltec prophecies in the Long Count and asked whether he could elaborate on the information. He gladly agreed. That is how I obtained such a complete and accurate account of what is currently happening.

Hugo told me that according to the predictions he had received from his teacher, Esteban, the transformation we were undergoing would have (unsurprisingly) four main steps:

Step 1: The Sphere of Fear

The first step is what we might call the Sphere of Fear. Fear of catastrophes, including pandemics, is an ancient one, based on what humanity has experienced in the past. It is inherent in all of us.

We may react to this fear in one of two ways. The first is by falling into the fourth underworld—the underworld of fear of change, laziness, and lack of discipline. It seems that the majority of people worldwide have done precisely this. They remain at home watching TV, hoping for a cure or vaccine to be found and normal life to resume. That life has gone and change is inevitable, but they won't face up to the fact. Instead, they cling to the world of the Fifth Sun and feel unnerved and stressed. So, on a collective level, we are seeing personal relationships starting to deteriorate, leading to increased domestic violence and even cruelty toward animals.

On the other hand, there are also people who have used their fear during this time of isolation as motivation for self-development. They have re-evaluated their lives and made what changes they could. They have sought information and taken up meditation and other spiritual practices. I myself have found that even though this has not been an easy time and the confinement and loss of freedom have been challenging, not being able to teach and travel has allowed me to go over the basics of my spiritual practice and take care of myself a little more.

Step 2: Economic Collapse

The second step in this transformation process would be, Hugo indicated, economic collapse on a level never seen in the modern world. Even as I write, millions of jobs have been lost around the world, and many specialists predict that the economy will continue to contract, with 2021 likely to be a time of economic upheaval.

In the same way as the Sphere of Fear, this process may be experienced in two completely different ways. Most people will react with fear and paralysis, hoping the government will support them or resolve the situation for them. Others will adapt, innovate, develop new income streams, become self-employed, and create new jobs for others, turning the situation into an opportunity to create new ways of supporting themselves, often ones that are more environmentally friendly. The ability to adapt is one of the highest qualities of people of the Sixth Sun, since this is a night Sun, and changes made in dreams manifest almost instantly. So these entrepreneurs and visionaries are moving with the times—into the Sixth Sun.

Step 3: A Great Technological Revolution

The third step in this great transformation is the one that, to me, offers both interesting and alarming possibilities. As already mentioned, the influence of the Sixth Sun began with a great technological revolution. To understand how this may progress, we briefly need to recap the characteristics of the day and night Suns:

Day Suns: During these Suns, just as when we are awake with our eyes open, we are focusing mostly on the outer world, which creates traditions and trends in the collective. It is easy for us to follow collective beliefs, such as God being an external energy that may hear our prayers or heal us. It is also easy for us to look to the outer world for satisfaction. This is where ambition, neediness, and the struggle to possess more come from.

Night Suns: Metaphorically speaking, during these Suns we are sleeping. Our external vision is temporarily suspended and we turn inward, listening to the inner voice that helps us to understand our psyche, our underworlds, and whether we are suffering or not. If we have undertaken spiritual development, we may have lucid dreams and understand that the origin of many of our waking experiences lies in our dreams. If we go beyond this, we may see the mind before the matter, our true nature behind our external appearance, and escape our reflection, or the illusion that is before us.

We have already seen that we are moving from a day Sun into a night one, and our shift of perception has been gradual, via technology. Today, computers and cell phones are many people's main interface with the world. But, as Hugo told me that afternoon, "As a result of solar activity and other important factors, technology will start to fail more and more frequently."

I have to say I personally experienced mobile networks and online banking becoming less reliable during the coronavirus pandemic. According to Hugo, this will continue to the point of complete failure. Spiritually speaking, this will show the people who have pinned all their hopes on a technological future that technology is not the solution. Furthermore, not being able to look outside themselves through technological devices will force them to look inward. This will be hard for many, but as a species, it could bring us great opportunities to adapt our collective mindset and finally see the truth that mind comes before matter. This may in turn bring an end to absurd ideas such as racism and gender inequity and enable us to work toward living in peace on our beautiful planet.

If this does not happen, and equality is not brought about between certain groups in power and the rest of the world, there are wild rumors that people trained in the knowledge and practices of ancient civilizations could be forced to work with the sun to destroy satellites, and other forms of technology that are controlling populations, and save the planet from annihilation.

Step 4: Days of Rage

Hugo mentioned that anger, violence, rioting, and looting would rise at the end of the Fifth Sun, the Sun of Rage. Of course in just the few months since our conversation took place, we have been witness to massive protests in the name of racial justice, and rioting, looting, and chaos increase with every passing day. We do not know where it will all end.

On the other hand, I am seeing a very different phenomenon taking place at the same time, and with a lot less publicity. During lockdown, many people have found peace, serenity, and joy in the simple things in life, from the patter of rain to small gatherings of friends and family. This is very encouraging and may ultimately lead to self-sufficient communities living in harmony.

In this, we can clearly observe the two Suns expressing themselves: the Fifth Sun through rage and destruction; the Sixth through quiet harmony. Ask yourself which Sun is influencing you more...

A Final Admission

Finally, Hugo mentioned one more prophecy. This was something I had heard many times before. It was that the authorities would begin to admit the existence of extraterrestrial races.

Some time later, NASA began to release material concerning UFO sightings. This confirmed once more that the ancient prophecies were true.

So, what did the Toltecs and Aztecs see written in the stars? What of the future? What is to come?

Chapter 4

A NEW CYCLE

The Long Count will finish with the lunar eclipse of May 26th, 2021, but its influence will extend at least up to the ceremony of the New Fire on November 24th, 2026.

Before then, several cosmic events will take place. As I write, the aphelion of July 2020, which coincides with a lunar eclipse, is still to come. The aphelion is the point in the orbit of the Earth at which it is farthest from the sun, so it is the darkest point. After the Earth, the second most powerful feminine force in the Toltec cosmology is Yohualpa, the night. Physicists describe darkness as a force that absorbs and transforms anything attracted to it, and although we have not realized it yet, when we are in deep Delta wave sleep, the darkness is purifying us.

Also, the sun in this position marks the recognition and rise of the divine feminine on this planet. Therefore, for the first time, Yohualpa will be selective: in other words, darkness will not cleanse those who refuse to accept gender equality and to respect the Earth. Consequently, there will be even more of a polarity between people who will adapt to the new conditions and start living healthily and in peace, and those who will cling to what they know and suffer adversity, not only as a result of the pandemic, but also their rigid and intolerant thoughts and feelings.

Later this year, the Catholic Church and other august institutions, in an attempt to hang on to power, will hold an important council and plan to allow women and other minorities to occupy top positions. However, a large sector of the population, including many important industrialists, will oppose these changes, causing friction around the world, since unless these measures are taken, recovery will be stalled not only by the pandemic, but also by the stagnant economy.

So, according to the prophecies, we will come to the lunar eclipse of 2021, which marks the beginning of the path through the heavens that leads to a new cycle.

THE PATH THROUGH THE HEAVENS

2021–2022: The First Heaven, the Heaven of the Moon, the Winds, and the Waters

This year we will be facing difficult challenges. First of all, the Black Wind of the North, which causes disease and economic crises, will continue to affect us, preventing the Blue Wind of the South from removing the thorns on our path.

However, if a good number of people start honoring the sacred feminine essence of the moon and the world of dreams, together with the purifying Red Wind of the West, we will start to witness more favorable conditions as well as the beginning of a rebalancing of masculine and feminine energies on the planet.

2022–2023: The Second Heaven, the Heaven of the Sun

This year will be particularly important in determining the influence of the next Sun on a human level. Of course, this will depend entirely on the decisions previously made by world leaders and the evolution of the collective consciousness of humanity.

According to the ancient Toltecs, there were two totally different suns: the sun of Quetzalcóatl, which encouraged people to develop spiritually; and the sun of Tezcatlipoca, which taught them harsh lessons through famine, misfortune, and war. This is similar to how the Egyptian solar goddess Sekhmet could bestow either pestilence, hardship, and misfortune or new life on the pharaoh and the Egyptian people.

This year, the collective consciousness of humanity will decide whether the sun of Tezcatlipoca will bring new pandemics or wars, or the sun of Quetzalcóatl will give us some respite. Therefore, this could be a year when we will be suffering another pandemic or a great war, or when we will start recovering.

2023–2024: The Third Heaven, the Heaven of Venus and the Pleiades

This year will be crucial in the development of a new world view, because inevitably women will seek equality and refuse to be treated as sex objects or baby factories any longer, due to the influence of the planet Venus.

In the Toltec culture, the "Venus of the sunset," the evening star, was considered the star of the *nahual*, the world of dreams. So, it will be this year that the hidden jewel of all traditions, the power of dreams, will be revealed to the world at large, and everyone will finally understand that we are made up of two parts: the conscious mind of our waking state and the unconscious mind of our dreams. We will begin dream training together, much as we go to yoga or meditation classes at present.

Sadly, the location of our sun this year with respect to the Pleiades will make people cling to the world of the Fifth Sun, which will cause a lot of deaths from war, economic depression, and crop failure due to pests. These people will be destined to come back in lineages that have adapted to the new order and whose genetics will make it easier for them to make the changes that they couldn't make in their previous life.

2023–2024: The Fourth Heaven, the Heaven of All Stars

This refers to the birth of a son/sun or illuminated being from a virgin mother. This is a story found in many cultures. In the Mexican version, Tonantzin, Mother Earth, was sweeping on the Hill of the Serpent, meaning the Earth, when suddenly a feather penetrated her, making her pregnant with Huitzilopochtli, the rising sun. When the moon and her sisters the stars knew that their mother was pregnant, they got jealous and decided to kill her in order to prevent the birth of the new sun. Mother Earth was very worried about this conspiracy, but then she heard a voice coming from her womb, saying, "Don't worry, I will defend you." So, when the moon arrived with her sisters to murder Mother Earth, the rising sun was born, and with a serpent of fire, he defeated the moon and stars. This symbolizes the triumph of the sun every morning over the moon and stars. It also symbolizes the triumph of masculine (day) Suns over feminine (night) Suns. As we have seen, these alternate, triumphing over each other in an ongoing cycle.

Metaphorically speaking, it will be during these years that the moon and stars will defeat the sun, marking the beginning of the reign of the feminine Sun, night, and the world of dreams.

Globally, this will see the establishment of a more sustainable, environmentally-friendly economic system. New forms of spirituality that include the Goddess and nature will emerge, as will more self-sustaining communities. Yet ironically, these developments will bring even more conflict, due to resistance by corporations and other old economic systems and ways of thinking.

2024–2025: The Fifth Heaven, the Heaven of Comets and Shooting Stars

For the ancient Mexicans, this heaven was representative of everything in the universe being in constant movement, a concept that seems normal nowadays. However, if we think about it, this heaven was formulated by cultures that existed thousands of years ago, and even 500 years ago the European view was still the geocentric one that everything revolved around the Earth.

For us, this will be a year of movement, an unpredictable one of sudden and spectacular change. It is predicted that the end of the year will see earthquakes, there will be a lot of suffering, and the whole world will be forced to change or to perish.

2025–2026: The Sixth Heaven, the Heaven of Movement

For the ancient Mexican cultures, the universe is movement created in the mind of the Black Eagle, Centeotl, or God, which is inevitably based on the number four. This year that cosmic movement will bring the 11th New Fire ceremony. This ceremony takes place every 52 years and marks the perfect alignment of Orion's Belt and the Pleiades, which is the start of a new cycle. This will take place on November 24th, 2026.

So, this will be the year when, either in a harmonious and peaceful way or forcibly, through upheaval and chaos, we will accept the new world of the Sixth Sun—a world of gender equality, a world of inner rather than outer focus, a world in which facing and solving the problems in our underworlds will be our only means of survival.

2026–2027: The Seventh Heaven, the White Heaven or the Heaven of the Moon

And so we will come to the first year of the Sixth Sun, the one that will have the greatest impact on the subsequent cycle.

This year is under the influence of the seventh heaven, and this heaven is ruled by the moon, so those who are able to lucid dream will not only be able to create their own reality from the dream state, but will also be capable of performing remarkable feats. This is the reason why this Sun is known as the return of the Quequetzalcóatl, those of precious knowledge, those who have awakened spiritually.

Chapter 5

THE ETERNAL CLOCK

One misinterpretation of the Mayan calendar was that the end of the Long Count meant the end of the world. But the end of a cycle doesn't necessarily mean great cataclysms or mass extinctions, although these have happened previously, as any search for information about the extinction of the dinosaurs will show. I wanted to write this chapter so it is clear that the end of the Fifth Sun isn't the end of the world, but a transition from one cycle to another, based on a mathematical and astronomical order that the ancient peoples of Mexico became specialist in.

Ever since I was young, I've heard the saying: "God must be a mathematician." Looking at the cosmos, this seems very true. The precision of celestial mathematics makes existence on this planet cyclical and repetitive, but at the same time new and wonderful. It is like being in an invisible prison of alignments that create similar conditions, but being free to do something different with them each time. The mathematician gives us free will.

FUTURE SUNS, FUTURE WORLDS

Based on the mathematical and cyclical nature of the universe, we can make some predictions for the distant future based on the position of the sun in relation to the Pleiades.

The Seventh Sun

In 6,625 years we will enter the Seventh Sun, which reigns from dawn to midday. Therefore, as it begins, as dawn breaks, we will conquer our weaknesses and go beyond our limitations to achieve things that are unimaginable to us now. This can also be foreseen by the numerology: the word for "seven" in the Náhuatl tongue means "the power of the two united energies," so this will be a Sun in which creativity will be a strongpoint.

The only problems that could arise are that as it is a predominantly masculine Sun, gender equality could be threatened, and as it will have some similarities with the Third Sun, with its excess of ego, there could be the possibility of war. However, as we say, "If you learn from the past, you won't repeat it," so it may be that the events of the Third Sun can be avoided rather than repeated.

The Eighth Sun

Thousands of years later, the Eighth Sun will arrive, the Golden Sun reigning from midday to sunset. Initially, it will be under the influence of masculine energy, and there will be a highly sophisticated technological culture, but little by little, under the influence of the number eight, which in Náhuatl means "the power of the bloodstream," more spiritual knowledge will appear. But because of the nature of the number eight and the legacy of the Fourth Sun, there could be great slaughter, as there was in ancient times when there was a change in beliefs. However, if we avoid this, there is the chance that we will see beyond the illusion of the material world and finally accept the existence of a spiritual world.

The Ninth Sun

When we take this great collective step forward, the Ninth Sun will come. This is known as the blue heaven. During this Sun, we will be able to connect with what many ancient traditions called our star guide. This didn't refer literally to a star in the cosmos, but to the stellar influence corresponding to our highest level of consciousness, so this means that we will finally reach enlightenment. However, those who will not accept it will perish.

This could also be a very complex Sun. It reigns from sunset to midnight, just as the Sun we are currently finishing, but, as it bears the number nine, the number of the underworlds, if in previous years we have not learned our lessons, this could be a Sun filled with destruction and suffering. But, as already mentioned, the cosmic clock sets the conditions, and it's up to us whether we make the most of them or not.

The 10th Sun

Following the movement of that eternal clock, we reach the midnight Sun again, which gives power to the feminine, but the number 10 is much more benevolent than the number six, and we could also benefit from the legacy of the return of the Quequetzalcóatl, so this Sun could be one filled with *tlazohteotl*, feminine strength and love.

This will lead the human race, within the following millennia, to the 10th heaven, the red heaven. This has been described as the return to the womb, where we, as a human being of Quetzalcóatl level, are conceived by two other human beings of Quetzalcóatl level, that is, two illuminated beings will invite another illuminated being to come into existence.

The possibilities of an Earth populated by such highly evolved beings are unimaginable.

The 11th Sun

And so the days repeat in the mind of the Eagle, and the Suns repeat, so we have a dawn Sun again, with masculine energy filtered this time by number 11, which indicates a new beginning, so I believe that during this Sun masculine energy could finally be used in a balanced and respectful way.

During the following millennia, we can also expect the beginning of the 11th heaven. This is the place where the gods live. All of us will have to accept the death of the gods, which has been forecast in several Eastern religions, but at the same time, we will have to accept our equality with the divine. This is one of the prophecies that I hope will be fulfilled during this Sun.

The 12th Sun

Though there are thousands of years to go, if I had the choice I would definitely choose to come back to the Earth of the 12th Sun, the midday Sun, the point at which there will be no shadows and the conditions will be perfect for a Golden Age.

During this age, the human race will enter the 12th heaven, the heaven of Ometecuhtli and Omecihuatl, Mr and Mrs Two, who symbolize the power of creation. At this level, the planet will evolve with us.

The 13th Sun

Finally, we will arrive at the 13th Sun, that is, we will enter into the mind of God, the Black Eagle, Centeotl, to create parallel universes and experience an expansion of consciousness difficult to describe.

We will end this brief prophetic tale at this point, where, as a species, we may choose to undertake more advanced lessons in other parts of the universe before the count returns to number one. As it will, for the process is cyclical, and when the Earth's position in the cosmos changes once more, everything will begin again from the very beginning, with the First Sun.

Thus our destiny is written in the heavens, which the ancient Toltecs were able to read.

Chapter 6

THE WHITE WOMAN'S AWAKENING AND AN ENCOUNTER WITH THE BLACK LADY

This time last year, Iztaccíhuatl, the white woman, Mexico's third highest volcano, awoke from a thousand-year-old dream and erupted, symbolizing the rising influence of the Sixth Sun. That influence is now unstoppable, and planetary consciousness is changing at an impressive rate.

THE FALL OF WOMAN

The main imbalance that we have been dragging with us from the Fifth Sun is the flintstone knife of injustice. This began with the dishonoring of the main feminine forces, the first being the Earth itself. Once considered sacred, as the years passed, our beautiful planet became viewed by the great majority as something inert that could be exploited, without respect or gratitude.

The second feminine force that fell into oblivion was the night, darkness. This was considered the origin of evil, even though the Bible states that it was from darkness that light was born. So the first mother, the cosmic mother, was ignored and forgotten as well. The moon, too, was dishonored, being considered a baleful influence that turned people into "lunatics" and inspired witches, pagans, and other dangerous and disreputable people who chose to remain in contact with the natural world.

There followed the fall of women in general, based on the biblical story of Eve tempting Adam and therefore being to blame for their expulsion from the Garden of Eden. Women were evil, not to be trusted, the weaker sex, fit only for having children and satisfying the desires of men. And the serpent, the ancient symbol of healing, evolution, and the Earth, became the source of sin and the downfall of humanity.

After the subjugation of the feminine by patriarchal religions, governments, and cultures, minorities of all kinds were also subjected to discrimination and abuse.

It was logical enough for a group that wanted to keep others in ignorance and subjugation.

But things are changing. At the beginning of the book we noted that the Aztecs' last *tlahtoani*, Cuauhtémoc, commanded them to keep their treasure safe for the Sixth Sun. They accepted that the consciousness of Central America would sleep for 500 years then reawaken. So, what was that consciousness? What was that treasure?

First of all, in those days there hadn't been a fall of the feminine in Central American culture. The prevailing cosmology affirmed that the primary energy, Centeotl, divided in two—the masculine and feminine forces, Ometecuhtli and Omecihuatl—and their children or guiding forces, who were later considered gods, had masculine and feminine names. The few that were only masculine had a feminine duality that had the same importance. Therefore, as the feminine forces had not fallen, neither had women. Worship of the Earth, the moon, and the night were as important as worship of the sun, and although later history talks of patriarchal societies, many of the conquistadors' own texts show respect for women and homosexuals and the existence of both male and female rulers and jaguar and eagle warriors.

The final piece of evidence that there was no fall of the feminine in Central America has to do with the fact that an imbalance of the Earth element is expressed through infections and pandemics. Logically, we can assume that this wasn't a problem for the ancient Mexicans, because it wasn't until the arrival of the Europeans that diseases such as syphilis appeared, and the smallpox that annihilated 90 per cent of the population. If there had been the same problem in Mexico, the Europeans would have found themselves exposed to epidemics that would have depleted their armies and populations. The fact that this did not happen shows there was equality between the male and female energies in America. This has not been the case for at least 500 years, but with the Sixth Sun, there must be a reconciliation and a rebalancing between the forces.

Unfortunately, some countries may oppose this, and these may be countries that have great economic strength, so wars could be fought for this equality in the economic arena. The collective consciousness of humanity might see this struggle as a misfortune. However, there will be individuals who will be able to separate their personal destiny from the one that most of humanity will experience by reconciling the masculine and feminine within themselves. This is a necessary first step toward the return of precious knowledge.

OUR DARK COSMIC MOTHER

To begin our adaptation to the Sixth Sun, we must recognize that in the Toltec tradition, the primary energy of creation, Centeotl, the Black Eagle, is considered primarily feminine, and is mainly represented by darkness, by the night. So, exactly as in the Bible, from darkness came light—darkness was the cosmic mother. Honoring her means honoring the energies and events of the night, for example the moon, which is the main ruler of change, including life and death on Earth, and of course sleep, which is the middle stage between the primary energy of creation and what we call matter.

So, the first force with which the ancient practitioners of nahualism, the people of power of ancient Mexico, made an alliance was the night. Although none recorded this friendship, the Spanish chroniclers mentioned that the Aztec rulers had as their main god Black Tezcatlipoca, or Smoking Mirror, which refers to a mirror of obsidian, a completely black volcanic stone. This god was later described as the force that brought fortune or misfortune and was associated with the unconscious, the so-called caves of the mind, hidden within.

The ancients had a much greater awareness of the primary consciousness that lies behind everything that exists. That is why so many old sayings, such as "If the mountain will not come to Muhammad, then Muhammad must go to the mountain," refer to natural features such as mountains having a consciousness in a living universe beyond the limits of human perception. Some people have experienced this through the healing power of plants, but you can experience it by simply opening your mind. Wake up to the midnight sun, remember that darkness allows you to look at what light hides, and your perception will expand. This is something that many people will develop naturally, and it will come to be seen as normal.

In Náhuatl cultures, the night is called Yohualli, but the consciousness behind the night, the black lady representing the cosmic mother, is called Yohualpa. (It is worth mentioning for those who have previously studied with me that the black lady can also be called Coatlicue, referring to the ability of the Earth to create and destroy. But the black lady representing the cosmic mother is the primary one.) In other cultures, like the Andean, this consciousness is known as the sacred black light, or Wilkan'usta. With the awakening of the white woman, we should be reconciled with the lady of the night, the black lady.

In the ancient world, there were certain practices to introduce people to this force. One of them consisted of walking from one spot to another and back again with a constant rhythm, striking the ground with the toes and heels. This activated energy centers in the feet, and if there were several people undergoing this initiation at the same time, the sound of their feet on the ground would resemble the sound of drums. Keeping the rhythm going, they would move back and forth at considerable speed, almost trotting, until the sound of their feet hitting the ground would make them fall into a kind of trance, an altered state of consciousness where they would access the space between their thoughts.

To contact the cosmic mother, they would perform this rhythmic movement for at least half an hour, then stand in one place and introduce themselves to the lady of the night in a respectful manner, saying, "I am [name], I am strength and power, I am source and emanation."

Then they would lower their head to share the emanation of their crown chakra, one of the energy centers of the body that in the Náhuatl cultures are called *totonalcayos*.

While sharing their energy with the night for a few moments, they would ask Yohualpa to present herself before them as the force that absorbed everything they no longer needed, removed their obstacles, and facilitated change, by saying, "Yohualpa, *xihualhui* [She-wall-we, 'come']," which is a way of respectfully calling the forces and energies in ancient Náhuatl.

They would wait a moment and move their eyes slightly outward to the periphery of their vision, that is, their left eye to the left and their right eye to the right. These were cultures accustomed to seeing the world from another perspective, and sometimes they would see a black silhouette in front of them, a woman's silhouette, like one of the Black Virgins that are so popular in certain areas and among certain power groups. Once this black lady had presented herself, the first thing the ancients would do was to offer her their problems, their illnesses, their blocks, their imbalances, and their past, saying, either in their mind or out loud, "I offer you my depression, poverty, hypertension, etc."

It is now well known scientifically that the color black absorbs, while light colors radiate. Therefore, it is logical that a dark force would start to suck up, like a vacuum cleaner or a black hole, everything these people didn't need, all their illnesses and problems, while at the same time retaining their friendship.

Subsequently, they would start walking again, trotting quickly to regain the trance state. Then they would stop again to call Yohualpa, but this time to ask her, as their cosmic creative mother, for the things that they wanted to come into their life.

This was the traditional practice, but as my work is to make ancient knowledge accessible to the modern world, I will share the way I do it now with my students.

CONNECTING WITH THE COSMIC MOTHER

This exercise will provide you with an alliance with the main feminine force, the cosmic mother, who will recognize you forever and give you the power to destroy what no longer serves you and create what brings you as close to your divinity as possible. As night is the energy you are connecting with, do this exercise at night.

✤ Sit comfortably in a quiet place.

✤ Begin by breathing in through your nose for a count of nine, the number associated with darkness and the night, and breathing out through your mouth for a count of nine. Breathing creates a harmonious rhythm throughout your body, just like trotting by alternating toes and heels.

✤ Repeat this breathing cycle 18 times—nine for the force of creation and nine for the force of destruction.

✤ In your mind, ask Yohualpa, the essence of creation, the darkness from which light came, to come to you as the force that releases, absorbs, and destroys by saying, "Yohualpa, *xihualhui* [she-wall-we]," or "Come," four times. If you want to shake a maraca or make a sound, then your mind will associate this sound with calling the energy.

✤ You will feel her coming, though maybe not at first, as a presence, a tingling sensation, or a variation in temperature. If you wish, you can try to see her as the ancients did, with your peripheral vision. Some of you will see her from the beginning and others over time, but the goal is not to have a visual experience, it is to introduce yourself to the cosmic mother.

❀ Present yourself and offer respect to this creative force by saying, "I am [name]. I am strength and power, I am source, and I emanate."

❀ In your mind, offer the cosmic mother your illnesses, problems, traumatic past events, "old Winds" or karma—everything you don't want in your life. There's no need to worry about this—cosmic forces don't think like we do, and it's not bad to offer the cosmic mother your suffering, since she created everything that we consider good and bad without judgment. So, offer all you can—the wider the offering, the more benefits you will receive. Don't forget to offer all the energy of the Fifth Sun that isn't useful to you in this transition. You can also offer things from the collective, such as pandemics, and other things that are making people suffer, so that the general transition to the new Sun is more harmonious.

❀ The creative forces are extremely respectful and won't do anything without your authorization, so give this now by saying, "I accept you taking my offering."

❀ Breathe in and out steadily, so that you can release everything you have offered—everything that has accumulated in your mind, in your soul, in your sleep, in your body. Let it all go. Feel it being sucked up by an energy vortex like a vacuum cleaner or a black hole.

It is being taken by a mother who is caring for a son or daughter who is healing and remembering.

❀ When you feel you have given everything, thank the cosmic mother and ask for part of your offering to be returned to you as a pure force of destruction, and for it to be deposited on your right side. This will fill gaps in your aura and empower you, so that later, just by closing your eyes and connecting with the darkness of your inner self, you can destroy your problems and those of the people you care for. This will be very necessary in the new Sun.

❀ Then repeat the process of breathing in through your nose for a count of nine and breathing out through your mouth for a count of nine.

❀ Do this 18 times in order to create a harmonious and synchronized rhythm with the strength of the night.

❀ And call Yohualpa again by saying, "*Xihualhui*," or "Come," four times.

❀ Feel her as a presence, tingling sensation, or variation in temperature, or, if you wish, try to see her. If you can't, don't worry. As I said before, this isn't the main purpose of the exercise.

❁ Once again, formulate your offering, giving the cosmic mother your problems, your anguish, and all the heavy things that come into your mind.

❁ When you have finished, say again, "I accept you taking my offering."

❁ Once again, feel the cosmic mother beginning to remove everything that isn't serving you. Remember to breathe in and out steadily so that you can release everything that has accumulated in your mind, in your soul, in your sleep, in your body.

❁ When you feel that you have been cleansed, give thanks and ask that part of the offering be returned to you as a pure force of creation and for it to be deposited on your left side. This will fill gaps in your aura and empower you, so that later you can use it to create—through your dreams, thoughts, your inner self, and your rituals—everything that you want to come into your life and the lives of those you care for, including a gentle and peaceful transition to the Sixth Sun.

Do this exercise as often as you can and you will be taking steps toward the new Sun. Remember that in the Fifth Sun, the creative force is seen as being outside you in the form of a god or gods who create for you, but in the Sixth Sun it must return to you, as must the power to heal. Your friendship with your dark cosmic mother will help you in these complex times, and the complete darkness of the underworld we are in, though it may be confusing, can nevertheless be the source of complete peace and the restoration of your power.

In the following chapters we will deal with the dream state and the other feminine forces with which we must begin to interact to become the Quequetzalcóatl, those of precious knowledge.

THE TRUE TREASURE
OF MEXICO

Our friendship with the lady of the night, or primal force, offers us many options for fully developing our power. In the previous chapter we mentioned accessing our inner being, the space between our thoughts, and in this one we will also address rituals, but where we will access the most creative power and control over our waking state is in our dreams.

When Hugo first met me, I knew little about the importance of sleep and its creative power. I remember that in his classes he insisted that we had to dream things before they would happen. I didn't believe this immediately, though I didn't doubt it either. I was simply disconnected from my dreams and what happened in them.

About a year later, he introduced me to his friend, another guardian of Mexican identity and heritage, Xolotl, who taught me, among many other things, a lineage of Toltec dreaming practices that he had documented.

I remember that when we first started those lessons, he recited a Teotihuacan saying: "A person who doesn't remember their dreams is one of the living dead, because they have no control over their life when they're awake."

I replied, somewhat dubiously, "But what you eat, think, do, and say is also important."

He said, "But that depends on what you dream."

I couldn't confirm or deny it, because I simply did not know. I had only just begun to explore my dreams. But when I thought about it, it was logical that the dream would come first, because that would explain why every language in the world had phrases like: "the woman of my dreams," "the house of my dreams," "my dream holiday," "my worst nightmare," and so on.

At that time, what I knew about sleep was pretty basic, as it is for most people: it's best to sleep for eight hours a night, uninterrupted, and undisturbed by dreams.

Sixteen years have passed since then, enough time to study the subject of sleep and become passionate about it. Through learning the lessons given to me by both my teachers and walking through the world of dreams, I could soon personally confirm the veracity of the ancient teachings. When your way of dreaming changes, your way of life changes too, and the Sixth Sun is taking us by the hand and leading us to that realization.

But there are always people ahead of their time. I learned that many business leaders were already practicing lucid dreaming, that the visionaries of Silicon Valley were using it to "dream up" new technologies, and that a multitude of people in high positions were using it as well. In fact, it wasn't anything special or strange and had been known about for a long time.

In the Bible, prophets had received messages in dreams and an angel had been sent to St Joseph in a dream to reassure him he could marry the Virgin Mary, as her child had come from God. Great historical figures such as Leonardo da Vinci had practiced the remembering the day backwards, which is one of the dreaming practices of the Mexican tradition, and other great artists had confirmed that they had dreamed of their creations before executing them in the "real" world. Even Einstein had stated that he had dreamed the Theory of Relativity, while the fathers of psychology, Freud and Jung, considered their sleep studies of fundamental importance.

In the face of all this evidence, it seems absurd to think that, with the exception of a few small groups of initiates, we have been disconnected from the dream world, a world, moreover, in which we spend a third of our lives.

For the ancient Mexicans, dream practices were at the heart of the teachings of power. It was always taught that the dreaming self had power over the waking one. Nahualism, a word popularized worldwide by the books of Carlos Castaneda, comes from the Náhuatl word *nahual*, which refers to the energetic body that we use when we sleep and will use when we die, and this in turn comes from the Náhuatl word *nehua*, which means "I." So, we can translate nahualism more or less as "the science of I." The part of ourselves that we use when we are awake, our conscious mind, is simply known as "the one we are with the sunlight."

The importance of sleep was recognized long ago by other cultures, such as the ancient Egyptians and Australian aborigines, and by spiritual traditions such as Buddhism and the Kabbalah. The power of dreams was considered the jewel of their mystic knowledge.

Why? I cannot speak for all these traditions, only the Mexican, but I can say that that is based on a cosmology of 13 heavens or dimensions that take us to a 14th: the world of the senses, material reality.

We have already spoken briefly of the heavens. In *The Dawn of the Sixth Sun*, I described them all in detail, but here I wish to focus on the seventh heaven, also called the white heaven, the place where the spirit of the moon lives and where dreams and daydreams take place.

If, from there, we jump forward to all of the heavens that follow, and that correspond to physical stars, suns, and moons, we will eventually reach the material world. Through this cosmology we will understand that dreaming is the most effective method of creation, simply because the world of dreams is closer to the primal energy of creation than to the material world. If we work there, our creations will manifest in at least half the time we might expect, although if we really try, they will manifest almost immediately.

THE SCIENCE OF SLEEP

I will now briefly explain what science currently knows about sleep. When I learned this, a long time after beginning my path as a Toltec dreamer, I was pleasantly surprised to find correlations between what had been established scientifically in the late 20th century and what had been handed down in the ancient dreaming tradition.

Sleep Cycles

There are several different types or cycles of sleep that we go through every night.

The Hypnagogic State

First of all comes the state we are in when falling asleep, the hypnagogic state. We can use this state to sow dreams to improve our life, as I will explain later on.

While falling asleep, we go through four different phases as our dominant brain waves change. We feel heavy, or rigid, and then we enter the famous sleep paralysis, the state that protects us from acting out our dreams and injuring ourselves. After that, our temperature drops by two degrees Celsius. That's why we cover ourselves up to sleep. Finally, with the sleep paralysis deepening, our respiratory muscles harden, slowing down our breathing and resulting in the classic breathing pattern by which we recognize that somebody is asleep. We lose consciousness on the way through these four steps and finally enter the Delta state, named after the brain wave that is dominant in this state and known as deep sleep.

Deep Sleep

In deep sleep, our consciousness simply contemplates the so-called bright darkness, the formless lights within our inner self. We are sleeping without dreaming, and this is when our body is healing and our hair and nails are growing. The ancient Mexicans called this Cochitzinco, the sacred place of sleeping without dreams.

Among the teachings on nahualism saved for the Sixth Sun, there is a technique called "The Blood Serpent," which we will also address later. This involves slowing down the cycles of our body so that we move though these four hypnagogic steps lucidly, noticing every step, and enter the Delta state still lucid. Science calls this state "awake Delta" and it offers a great opportunity to meet the lady of the night, the energy of creation, who may make shapes, for example what we call the eye of Tezcatlipoca and is otherwise known as the eye of the soul, the eye of Horus, or the third eye. If we see it, we can use it to look in any direction we wish. Since it is made of the creative force, we can use it to see ourselves as we wish to be— healthy, happy, and so on.

Also, in the Delta state we may see the true nature of our spirit, mind before matter, and so cease to identify with our human form and challenge the concepts of solidity we have been taught.

The REM State

Approximately at 40 to 45 minutes in, our sleep cycle will change, and we will enter the REM (rapid eye movement) state. Seeing rapid eye movement beneath closed lids is how we know someone is dreaming. This cycle will last approximately 15 minutes.

The sequence of 45 minutes of deep sleep and 15 minutes of dreaming will be repeated three or four times, depending on how many hours we sleep. But something else occurs around halfway through: the order is reversed, so we have 45-minute REM cycles that end with 15 minutes of deep sleep, and they will alternate until we wake up.

This is the reason why the great traditions of the world advise that one way to dream lucidly is to "cut the night," which means waking up three or four hours after going to sleep and waiting for about 15 to 20 minutes to break the pattern before going back to sleep again. The Toltec tradition advises carrying out the "Blood Serpent" exercise of slowing down the bodily cycles, going through the four hypnagogic phases lucidly, and falling asleep while still lucid. This induces Gamma brain waves, which are very healing.

The Hypnopompic State

Another sleep cycle in which we can work to create our destiny is when we start to wake up, which is called the hypnopompic state. In this state, as in the hypnagogic, we can sow dreams. We can also go back over the night, recapitulating what happened, which will help us to remember our dreams.

REMEMBERING DREAMS

This first exercise will help you to remember your dreams. Remembering your dreams is important preparation for dream work.

❋ When you wake up in the morning, before moving, while still in the hypnopompic state, go through the night backwards.

❋ Start by asking yourself: "What just happened? Was I dreaming?"

❋ You may not remember anything at first and then the memories may return. When you remember something, ask yourself what happened before it.

❋ Continue in this way until you have remembered the maximum eight dreams of the night.

❋ Then you may record them, either verbally, or in a dream journal, or however you wish.

This process is very useful, as it will demonstrate to your *nahual* that its messages are important. Continue over time and you will begin to notice changes in your way of dreaming and then changes in your way of life, and you will be one of the pioneers using the ancient science of sleep, the treasure that was kept for this time.

As the Sixth Sun is a midnight Sun, it is one in which the Toltec dreaming practices may reach a high point of development and sophistication. It is time for them to come into their own. In the Fifth Sun we have created an imbalance between the masculine and feminine in both the waking and dreaming worlds. The first hours of deep sleep are considered the feminine part of sleep, and the dreams in the REM state the male part. If you are just starting out as a dreamer with this book, then both are unbalanced and lacking in you. It is time for us all to sow new dreams and rebalance the forces of creation.

As I write, I feel quite excited. I feel I am carrying out the wishes of the last ruler of the Aztecs and sharing their hidden treasure with the world.

SOWING DREAMS

What does sowing dreams mean? To put it simply, it is making dream suggestions to our unconscious mind while in the hypnagogic or hypnopompic state in order to obtain a particular result in the waking world. That is the most obvious way to see it.

If we look below the surface, however, it is the main way of empowering the people of the Sixth Sun. That is, during this transition, of empowering ourselves.

I learned that dreams followed ancient patterns. These were handed down, just as family patterns were. The story remained the same, though the features might be adapted over time. If my great-grandfather dreamed of being chased by a horse, for example, I would dream of being chased by a plane or a car. Same story, different symbol.

Sowing dreams tells our unconscious mind, in an act of absolute power, that we no longer wish to dream the same way. We want new symbols, new archetypes, new stories, new results. We want to dream a new dream and live a new life.

In ancient times, this practice was called Mexicatzin. In my second book, *The Toltec Secret*, I taught how to sow dreams for health, abundance, and spiritual growth, but now, at this crucial time, I will teach you how to sow a dream specifically for empowerment and balance in the transition to the Sixth Sun and for the creation of a new wonderful era.

The Night and the Moon

As we learned earlier, some of the feminine forces that have been denigrated in the waking world are the night and the moon. But they are some of the most important feminine forces that will be used in forthcoming years in sowing dreams, for the night can remove our problems, and the moon can bring good fortune as well as disgrace.

In the Toltec tradition of nahualism, our dream body, or *nahual*, transforms into archetypes, which can take the form of animals, plants, and elements. These will look separate from us, but are really transformations of our own dream body.

SOWING A DREAM FOR THE SIXTH SUN

When learning to sow dreams, we normally start with animal archetypes. The one that represents the night is the black panther, and the moon is represented by the eyes of the panther being completely white, without iris or pupil, which means our unconscious mind can catch the attention of our conscious mind, and the energy behind the moon and the night will bring our dreams to life.

Big changes will happen in our lives when we encounter archetypes in our dreams.

This exercise is to be done at night before going to sleep, prior to the hypnagogic state.

❀ Sit comfortably in your bed.

❀ Dreams are sown through five different cycles of breathing. First, to destroy the energy of the problems you have in the waking world, close your eyes and turn your head to the left. Keeping in mind what you wish to destroy (you may include several things in one request), inhale through your nose and exhale through your mouth 13 times, destroying with your breath all the energy that gave these things life.

❀ Now, without opening your eyes, turn to the right to destroy the dreams that created these problems (even through you do not remember them) and the ancient patterns that led you to dream like this. Do this in the same way as before, by inhaling through your nose and exhaling though your mouth 13 times.

❀ The third step is to look up, as if you were staring at the cosmos, which for the ancient peoples was the seed of everything. And then transform any cosmic or planetary energy that is creating these problems in the same way, by inhaling through your nose and exhaling though your mouth 13 times.

❋ Look down, still with your eyes closed, and imagine that on your thighs is a bucket filled with water or an obsidian mirror in which you are reflected. (Just imagine it for now, but on one of the more advanced courses that I teach around the world, we really do it with water or a mirror.) The purpose of this breathing cycle is to make your reflection disappear. Do it in the same way, by inhaling through your nose and exhaling though your mouth 13 times.

❋ Now, see your reflection in the imaginary mirror disappear and, in its place, see a black panther with white eyes, representing the night and the moon. Your conscious mind will register this as your *nahual* or dream body, which now has the night and the moon's power and friendship.

❋ Look forward once again, without opening your eyes, and visualize the reflection of the panther with white eyes rising to your belly button, which is the place in which, according to the ancient tradition, our energetic body is located and from which we take off to the seventh heaven, the land of dreams.

❋ The fifth breathing cycle consists of inhaling through your nose and taking the air deeper into your lungs, then contracting the muscles around your belly button as you would in crouches or sit-ups, before exhaling.

❀ Do this 12 times and then, the 13th time, inhale and contract the muscles around your belly button as before, and as you exhale, observe your *nahual*, in the form of the panther with white eyes, leaving your belly button to go to the land of dreams.

❀ Lie down in bed, ready to sleep, and in your mind tell your feet, which are the part of your body that takes you where you want to go: "Take me to dream with the panther with white eyes. Take me to destroy my problems."

❀ Name each problem in your mind and what you want to have instead, and then repeat it while visualizing the panther moving to your right, to the land of dreams.

❀ Continue doing this until you fall asleep. In this way, the strength of the night and the moon will be active in your sleep and unconscious mind, destroying what you don't need and creating new patterns.

❀ The next step is that while you are repeating your suggestions, you should try to be aware of the process of falling asleep—going through the four phases of feeling heavy, feeling rigid, feeling your temperature drop, and finally feeling the rhythm of your breathing change. You may be surprised by your own snoring and will realize you are completely lucid with the mind of an ancient Toltec dreamer. But if you do fall asleep before that, it doesn't matter, since the seeds of destruction and creation have already been sown.

❦❦❦❦❦❦❦❦❦❦

I suggest that you do this dream-sowing exercise for the Sixth Sun at least twice a week and on two other days you do other exercises, such as the ones on the following pages. So, you spend four nights a week working in your sleep and the other three nights resting. Does that seem fair?

❦❦❦❦❦❦❦❦❦❦❦❦❦❦

THE BLOOD SERPENT

This exercise will help you to fall asleep lucidly and contact the lady of the night. It should also be done during the hypnagogic state before sleep.

❉ Sit comfortably in your bed. You are going to do a series of breathing exercises that will help you to synchronize with the moon.

❉ Inhale through your nose, counting in your mind to seven, and exhale through your mouth, again counting to seven. Seven is the number that synchronizes with the moon, since each phase of the moon lasts for seven days. Do this seven times, which will align you with the waning moon (it doesn't matter what phase of the moon it is currently), and state in your mind what you wish to remove from your life through this exercise.

❀ Now, repeat the breathing cycle, which will align you with the new moon, and state that you will create things that you do not yet know through this exercise.

❀ Do a third breathing cycle, which will align you with the waxing moon, and think of the things that exist in your life that you wish to grow and develop.

❀ Finally, do a fourth breathing cycle, which will align you with the full moon, and state that you wish to achieve your highest potential in life.

❀ Now you have done four cycles of seven, so have reached the number 28, the number of the lunar cycle. Begin visualizing that your blood is turning into a snake, the ancient symbol of healing and wisdom. Observe this snake winding its way through your veins and arteries, removing everything that isn't useful anymore, rejuvenating you, and giving you wisdom.

❀ Lie down and continue visualizing the blood serpent going through your body and healing you, then take it to your heart. For the ancients, the heart was the point of contact between the *tonal* and the *nahual*, the waking world and the world of dreams. Visualizing or feeling the snake in your heart, command that your heartbeat and all the cycles of your body slow down ... more and more ... and when you feel heavy, count to one.

❀ Visualize the snake in your heart again, move it more slowly, and command that your heartbeat and all the cycles of your body slow down ... more and more ... and when you feel heavier, count to three. If you fall asleep now, you should be able to do so while still lucid.

❀ Take the serpent back to your heart again, and command your heartbeat and all the cycles of your body to slow down even more ... until you begin to feel rigid. Command yourself to enter sleep paralysis. Count to four. Then five and six. By now your fingers and toes will begin to feel quite rigid, and you will become aware of the process of falling asleep.

❀ Once more take the serpent to your heart and command that everything slows down even further ... until you begin to feel a slight change in temperature. If you wish, as you are still lucid, you can heat up areas of your body if necessary or imagine a gentle breeze cooling you down. Count to seven. Then eight and nine.

❋ Finally, at the point of falling asleep, take the snake to your heart again and ask that all the cycles of your body slow even further, so that the sleep paralysis becomes deeper. You are now heading toward the land of dreams, and it may require a major effort to breathe slowly and deeply and stay lucid, but keep going. Keep counting until you reach 13. Then just concentrate on the sound of your breathing. That may convince you that you are really asleep, although still lucid, still aware.

❋ After concentrating on your breathing, simply confirm that you are entering the Delta state lucid.

❋ There, try to still your mind and enter a state of meditation. Crossing your eyes (with your eyes closed) and looking toward your nose often helps. Then raise your eyes, looking toward your third eye, in the center of your forehead. You may see the lights in the darkness (which are different colors for everyone) that signify the presence of the lady of the night and her creative power inside you in the space where there are no thoughts.

❋ Many things may then happen:

~ The lights may begin to form shapes, the main one being the eye that in the Toltec tradition is called the eye of Tezcatlipoca. This brings good fortune, so if you see it, leave the meditation for an instant and determinately say, "See me [as you wish to be, for example happy]."

~ Two eyes or the faces of animals or people may appear in these lights. If you see them, they are the materialization of your energetic doppelgänger, to whom you will determinately say, "Dream me [as you wish to be]."

~ The silhouette of the lady of the night may also manifest. If so, reaffirm your friendship with her.

~ If suddenly these lights become clear, you are entering what Buddhists call "clear light" or your true "Buddha nature," which could also be described as Quetzalcóatl or Christ Consciousness.

~ If they become dark and you see a small grid, you are seeing what the ancient Mexicans called "the spider web of the collective dream." In other traditions, this is "bright darkness" or "the quantum field." It is where you may tell the cosmic grid what you want to create.

❀ Every time that your mind takes you away from the meditative state, look toward your nose again and then back up toward your third eye and remain in that position until you fall back into the meditative state. But don't be hard on yourself if you simply fall asleep—you may have already changed your life completely by contacting the primal creative force inside yourself.

I recommend you do this exercise once a week. It will empower the feminine side of your dreams.

Blossom Dreams

The way to empower the masculine side of our dreams is to fall asleep and dream lucidly. The ancient Toltecs called a lucid dream a "blossom dream." Becoming lucid is only the start, though. After that, we enter what is scientifically known as "super lucidity" and begin to move through our dream at will with determination and purpose.

As mentioned earlier, the correct time for dreams is the second half of the night, after sleeping for three or four hours.

BLOSSOM DREAMING

For this exercise, you don't have to sow a dream in the hypnogogic state or visit the bright darkness, just fall asleep as normal. What you do have to do is wake up after three or four hours. What I do when I want to do this is drink large quantities of water before sleeping. Then I will be certain to get up to go to the bathroom.

❊ When you wake, beware of going straight back to sleep. Wait for a reasonable time, between 15 and 20 minutes.

❊ Do "The Blood Serpent" exercise (*see p.98*) again, counting to 13 and going through the four stages of falling asleep while still conscious.

❊ This time, instead of entering the Delta state, the sacred place of sleeping without dreams, you want to enter the Gamma state and dream. Again, with your eyes closed, look toward your nose, then up toward your third eye, and then relax your eyes completely. Eventually they will start to move, powered by electric impulses, and you will enter the REM state and can begin to create your dreams.

What should you dream? I can give you a few recommendations, such as making the panther with white eyes chase and destroy your problems. The dream archetype of destruction is Fire. Therefore, if you create representations of diseases or problems, burn them. The archetype of purification is rain, so if people or situations are troubling you, make it rain over them. Let the beneficial Winds blow through your dreams: the Red Wind purifies; the Blue Wind removes thorns from your path; the Yellow Wind brings whatever you need in life. Flowers signify the manifestation of beauty in your life and what you wish for. In my book *The Toltec Secret*, you can find other dream archetypes that you can use in your lucid dreams.

You can also do things that are impossible in the waking world, such as flying, breathing underwater, or walking through walls. When you do these things, you will be loosening the grip of the idea that the world is solid. For the dream body or the right hemisphere of the brain, the limits of the waking world do not exist.

Aim to dream lucidly at least once a week to keep your life in order and open up to what you consider impossible.

Chapter 8

ALIGNING WITH MOTHER EARTH

If you have been following closely, you will realize we have been journeying through the heavens. We started with the cosmic mother in the 13th heaven, passed through the dream world in the seventh, and have now arrived in the 14th, which actually isn't considered a heaven, because it is where we are now, on Mother Earth, in the world of matter.

Up to now, it is undeniable that the Earth has been neglected by the vast majority of people. Although she is a living ecosystem, she has been treated as merely the backdrop to our personal dramas. Having said this, I strongly disagree with the arrogant opinions of people who claim that we are destroying the Earth. To start with, if something doesn't exist in the Earth's dream, it cannot take place without her consent. As a conscious being, the Earth has the capacity to decide what happens here in accordance with the cosmic math of the universe. And she is now moving to a different point in that universe, which implies that she will take with her those who want to join her and will let go of those who decide to stay where they are.

In Náhuatl, the Earth is known as Tlalli Tonantzin Coatlicue. I mention this here because we need to understand her the way the ancient Toltecs did. *Tlalli* is soil that is prepared for sowing, i.e. is moist and fertile. *Tonantzin* is our venerable mother, and she is important because, like the cosmic mother, she can give or take life from anything that exists on her body. Therefore, it is time to recognize that the Earth is in control and it is actually humanity that has the problem.

All the ancient chronicles indicate that the Fifth Sun will end with earthquakes, that there will be a lot of suffering and pain, and that the whole world will perish, though this doesn't refer to death but to change. Those who decide to stay here and move into the next Sun will need the approval of Mother Earth in order to do so. She will perform a cleansing in many different ways. She has already started. The proof is in the coronavirus pandemic, the possibility of subsequent ones, the economic collapse, the recent earthquake in Mexico City, and the growing probability of the outbreak of a war aimed at the destruction of the old order and the establishment of a new one.

In order to survive, not as a species, but simply as human beings who want to reach the New Fire of 2026, we must stop looking at the Earth as if it were a hotel and instead start recognizing her as a long-suffering mother who has patience with those who inhabit her, but who also has the potential to both create and destroy. The moment she has to do away with whatever isn't necessary, she will do so without hesitation.

THE DUAL ENERGIES OF THE EARTH

For the ancient Mexicans, the Earth had two important names and qualities, which I am going to describe in Náhuatl, since the language preserves the essence of what is being described. However, we don't need to remember these words during our practices.

The first name, Tlazolteotl, refers to *tlazolteotl*, the energy that carries away everything that is old and useless and recycles it.

The second name, Tlazohteotl, refers to *tlazohteotl*, "the precious essence that gives life to everything." In our modern limited language, this might be what we understand as love.

These two polarities have always existed simultaneously on Earth, and they are known as life and death. When *tlazolteotl* acts, it is able to create anything from a small disease or minor accident to a tsunami in order to carry away people whose vibration doesn't have an evolutionary purpose here. The other essence, *tlazohteotl*, is always creating, always giving life. However, it even creates what we consider evil, and helps people to create that too.

Now, for the first time, I am going to reveal the way these energies work together. I need to point out that I'm not sure about the measurement method the Earth uses, but I know that it is definitely associated with gravity. The Earth is wise enough to weigh the amount of heavy energy in us. Heavy energy may be accumulated on our left side, from the *tonal* waking state, or in our right, from our dreams and ancestors. Both will be measured, and those who carry a larger amount of heavy energy on their right side, corresponding to *tlazolteotl*, and so have an endless number of things they have not let go of, will be distinguished from those who carry a higher amount of heavy energy on their left side, corresponding to *tlazohteotl*, and are always willing to help others.

We may recall that this is similar to Egyptian mythology, according to which a deceased individual's heart was weighed against a feather to determine whether or not they could transcend to another life.

This is the process the Earth is carrying out at present: she is weighing our energy to determine whether we stay here or not during this shift. The most important phase of this measuring period will start with the eclipse of May 2021 and will extend up to the New Fire in 2026, when it will be determined who will move forward with the new Sun and who will depart.

Most people will never know this process is taking place, since they will experience a seemingly random synchronization of events. Those of us who are aware of it can choose to be reconciled with the Earth, to connect with her, honor her, and move with her into the Sixth Sun as abundant, prosperous, and evolved beings.

In a physical sense, it is our legs and feet that are our connection with the Earth, and if we observe the ancient Mexican sculptures that represent Mother Earth, we will see that most have either one foot or the other forward. This is also evident in the Egyptian statues of the goddess Sekhmet, who, in similar dualistic fashion, gave the pharaoh either abundance and good fortune or pestilence and problems.

In the Mexican tradition, since our legs and feet are our connection with the Earth and also represent our underworlds, these are the parts of our body that we have to move in order to make changes in our life, create new relationships, and communicate with Mother Earth. To connect with her energy *tlazolteotl*, the energy that carries away everything we no longer need, we simply have to put our right leg in front of our left one. This indicates the way the energy is flowing, but we will still need to indicate, with our hand, where to remove the heavy energy from.

To understand this, we will briefly study the ancient Toltec *totonalcayos*, or chakras.

The Totonalcayos

There are seven *totonalcayos*, or energy centers, as follows:

1. *Colotl*, "scorpion," color: black; located in the coccyx. This is where all our destructive personal and ancestral patterns reside.

2. *Ihuitl*, "feather," colors: red and white; located in the genital area. All our sexual patterns accumulate here as well as all our heavy creations. Our creations must be as light as a feather so that our Quetzalcóatl energy, the Mexican equivalent to kundalini, may move upward.

3. *Pantli*, "flag," color: white; located in the navel. A flag is the symbol of the number 20. There are 20 day glyphs in the calendar, and the glyph of the day we were born on, together with a number from 1 to 13, sets our destiny in life. So, this center determines whether our path to fortune is open or closed. When it is blocked, we cannot receive either abundance or motherly care. But we can work with it to transmute the vibration of our birth and turn challenges into opportunities.

4. *Xochitl*, "flower," color: red; located in the chest, right behind the thymus. For the ancient Toltecs, blooming meant illumination, enlightenment. According to them, everything that manifested in a beautiful way, without suffering, bloomed. So we can work with this center to live our best, most beautiful life. It is also the center in charge of regulating the immune system.

5. *Topilli*, "scepter," color: blue; located in the throat. This is the center of self-esteem, power, and arrogance, the place where we can say mean words, or wise ones that express true power.

6. *Chalchiuhuitl*, "jade," color: green; located at the forehead, the place where the four Waters live. As you will remember, Water that does not fall, or drought, shows us what we lack. Water in the form of hail destroys and creates our destructive patterns. Water that floods represents all the excesses in our life that harm us. Finally, Water falling as rain makes things grow in a balanced way.

7. *Tecpatl*, "flintstone knife," colors: red and black; located at the crown. This where we find the influence of the previous Suns, which determines the amount of heavy energy we are carrying and where, which in turn will determine whether we stay on this planet and enter the Sixth Sun or not.

CONNECTING WITH THE DUAL
ENERGIES OF THE EARTH

Do this exercise regularly, at the same time of day, which can be anytime, as long as it's in daylight.

❀ Find a place where you feel at peace—in a park, at home, and so on.

❀ Inhale through your nose, counting in your mind to seven, and exhale through your mouth, again counting to seven.

❀ Once you have finished, take a step forward with your right leg, so that you can access *tlazolteotl*, the Earth energy that carries away everything that is no longer useful and recycles it.

❀ Consider what you want to let go of in your life and which of the energy centers it comes under. If you have problems in all of them, you may repeat the process for each of them. If that isn't the case, repeat the process for at least the first four centers and the seventh, the one of the flintstone knife, which is a must.

❀ As you are working with your right side, now close your right fist. According to the ancient cosmology, each of our fingers is connected to a phase of the moon: the dark of the moon (the thumb); the new moon (the little finger); the waning moon (the third finger); the full moon (the middle finger), and the waxing moon (the first finger). Thus by closing your fist, you are concentrating the power of the five lunar phases as catalysts of change.

❀ If you decide to start with the coccyx, put your fist on this point while in your mind you offer Tlazolteotl all your personal and family patterns that aren't useful anymore. Then say, "I accept you taking my offering." You will literally feel that energy is being pulled down both your legs, as if they were two heavy tree trunks rooting themselves in the earth. Inhale, exhale, and let go of it all.

❀ Once you feel you are ready, you may, though this is an optional step, put your fist on your genital area and offer all your negative sexual patterns and "heavy creations." Say, "I accept you taking my offering." Inhale and exhale until you feel a total cleansing that goes all the way down your legs to your roots.

❀ Now, put your fist on your navel center and offer all the problems you have with your mother, with infections, and with finances, so that the umbilical cord is opened up again and you can receive care and abundance. Once again, say, "I accept you taking my offering." Inhale and exhale until you feel a total cleansing that goes all the way down your legs to your roots.

❀ Continue placing your fist on your energy centers (the chest is also optional) and sending all your heavy energy down for the Earth to absorb and recycle during the shift to the next Sun.

❀ Whatever you have been releasing, the last step is fundamental, since the prophecy talks about a group of more conscious and evolved people. Therefore, with your fist on your crown chakra, release all the problems you and the human species are facing now as a result of the legacy of the previous Suns, so that both you and humanity can make the shift to the next Sun, having resolved all the remaining problems of the previous ones.

❀ Once you have completed the process with your right leg forward, put both legs together, balancing the powers of creation and destruction.

❀ Then take a step forward with your left leg, so you can access the precious Earth energy that brings life and happiness. Repeat the process above with all the centers that you consider necessary, but this time, place your left fist on the relevant area, and instead of asking the Earth to remove what you don't want, ask for what you do want. For example, if you go to the sexual area, you could ask to have discipline, strength of will, and the ability to accept change. Ask Tlazohteotl to make this energy move upward through your legs and to fill your genitals with it.

❋ At your navel, ask for abundance and care from Mother Earth.

❋ At your chest, ask for the blossoming of your life.

❋ At your forehead, ask for the rain that makes everything blossom in a beautiful way.

❋ When you reach the last center, your crown, ask for the energy of the Sixth Sun, the energy of someone who has escaped from the illusions of gender, race, and other differences in their life and in their energy, and who is seeing the mind rather than the matter in everyone and everything.

❋ When you have finished, put your legs together again, and put your hands together too, and say, "*Ometeotl*. May both of my polarities align harmoniously with the energy of the new Sun."

Do this exercise once or twice a week, depending on your needs, but believe me, a person who has roots in the earth is protected by the Earth. And the Earth will smooth their way for them, because those roots are the beginning of the flower of enlightenment.

We have almost completed our basic preparations for the new Sun. Of course, there is much more to be said, but if you have come this far, you will have stopped living in the past and be aligned to the future.

The only things left to consider are the four elements: Fire, Earth, Water, and Wind. We have mentioned them briefly elsewhere, but now we will look at them more closely.

THE FOUR ELEMENTS

In the ancient Mexican tradition, there are in fact four Fires, four Earths, four Waters, and four Winds, all of which feature in many other traditions around the world.

The Four Fires

We will begin with the Fires, as they are the strength behind our immune system, the part of our body that has been the most compromised in the first phase of this transition.

As you may remember, the elements have gender. Three of the Fires are male and one is female.

The four Fires are:

1. **The Young Fire** *(Xiuhtecuhttli)*: This is the wild Fire that burns furiously, races away, and ends up consuming acres and acres. It is the Fire behind our vitality, our strength. Our immune system is stimulated by this Fire, which is also the Fire of war, to destroy viruses, bacteria, and cancer.

2. **The Female Fire** *(Chantico)*: This is considered the Fire of home, the one that cooks with love, keeps the home fires burning, and brings the warmth of tenderness. Our immune system urgently needs this Fire to upgrade its vibration and make the Earth a place where we feel at home without the need to fight.

3. **The Ancient Fire, the Fire of Knowledge** *(Huehueteotl)*: This is the wise Fire that many cultures say the gods gave to humanity. It is the one that lights the uncertain path through the underworld of complete darkness and allows us to see the way forward.

4. **The Solar Fire** *(Tzontemoc)*: This is associated with great success in any area we take it to.

CREATING A STRONG IMMUNE SYSTEM

This exercise will help you to create an immune system that works with the four Fires, as it always should have. Do this exercise in daylight, ideally at noon, to benefit from the strength of the sun.

The right side of our body corresponds to the masculine and the left to the feminine. Therefore, masculine forces are summoned with the right hand and feminine forces with the left hand.

❀ Sit down comfortably in a pleasant place, ideally outside in the sunshine or in a place where sunshine is streaming through a window.

❀ Inhale through your nose while counting to 13, then exhale through your mouth while counting to 13, as this is the number that represents the sun and Fire. Do this 13 times.

❀ Once you have finished, make four offerings as follows:

~ Hold out your right hand, palm upward, and blow across your palm, offering your good energy.

~ Offer your good dreams in the same way.

~ Then feelings.

~ Then actions.

✿ When you have finished, call the Fire, saying, "Young Fire, *xihualhui*," four times and extending your right hand.

✿ You will feel the energy arrive, the spirit of this Fire— mind before matter, as always. When you feel it, close your fist, take it to your thymus gland, and empower your immune system with it, so it has the strength to battle viruses, bacteria, and cancer cells, and becomes invincible.

✿ When you feel that you have charged it enough, change to your left hand and make the same four offerings to the Female Fire, *Chantico*.

✿ Invite it to come to you by saying, "Female Fire, *xihualhui*," four times and extending your left hand.

✿ Allow the spirit of this Fire to arrive. When you are filled with its love and tenderness, close your fist, take it to your thymus, and raise the vibration of your immune system. Know that with this love, the mind cannot attack itself and has no need to fight, and the vibrations of viruses, bacteria, and people will all rise to this vibration of love. Another option is to take your fist directly to your heart to bring this precious essence into all your relationships.

✸ Next, with your right hand, make your four offerings to the Ancient Fire and then invite it to come to you in the same way as before.

✸ When its spirit arrives, close your fist and take it to the thymus as well, so it fills your body with wisdom and enables you to navigate through the pandemics and the ups and downs of life in a balanced and wise way.

✸ Finally, hold it out in front of you, so it lights the path that now is in darkness and shows you how to reach the new Sun in the best way.

THE SOLAR FIRE

The fourth Fire, the Solar Fire, works differently. So, do this exercise between dawn and midday to draw in the sun's energy.

✸ It simply consists of looking at the sun, either through a window or directly. If you have the time, show yourself to it as you did to the lady of the night (*see pages 75 and 98*).

✸ Begin to draw in the sun's energy—drinking the sacred, as the ancient Toltecs put it—as if you were smoking it: draw it in, swallow it, take it to your thymus, so that it begins to shine, and then exhale the air, while keeping the solar Fire within you. Do this 13 times.

With these exercises, I assure you, you will have a strong immune system, ready for what is to come. Another of the Aztec treasures saved for this moment in time.

The Four Winds

Three of the Winds are also male and one is female. Then the Earths and Waters are almost fully female, balancing the elemental system.

The Winds are:

❀ *The Black Wind of the North*, which is the one that brings misfortune and has been quite busy lately.

❀ Because of the misfortune, its influence cancels out that of the *Blue Wind of the South*, which removes thorns from our path.

❀ And minimizes the influence of the *Yellow Wind of the East*, which brings good fortune.

❀ Therefore, our hope lies in the *Red Wind of the West*, the female one, which purifies.

WORKING WITH THE RED WIND

The way to work with the Red Wind is quite simple. Do this exercise once a week for purification.

❀ Inhale through your nose for a count of nine, then exhale through your mouth for a count of nine. Nine is the number of the Winds as well as the number of the night.

❀ With your left hand, make four offerings to the female Wind, the Red Wind of the West.

❀ Invite it to come saying, "Female Wind, *xihualhui*," four times.

❀ When you feel it arrive, take it around your head to clear your thoughts and experiences from your heart and soul, then send it to your liver to purify yourself of diseases and problems, and finally let it settle for a moment in your belly button to help your dreams come true.

❀ Next, direct it to your house. Visualize it cleaning the kitchen and the bathrooms, boosting the health of those who live there. Then take it to the dining room, which is the area where we enjoy the benefits of our working life, then the living room, which we share with our friends and partners, and our bedrooms and the rooms of the other members of our family. It will clear the house, and, believe me, afterward, when you call it, it will come back through a window without you noticing it.

❀ If you aren't tired yet, take it through your neighborhood, especially around the areas where you know there are problems, since the feminine vibration can take care of any disorder we may cause.

CONCLUSION:
TODAY AND
TOMORROW

I n spite of all the information I have presented here and all the challenges we are facing, there is still hope.

First of all, I want to emphasize yet again that for many traditions, like Dream Yoga, nahualism, and the Kabbalah, dreaming is the crown jewel that had to be rediscovered. For me, it is magical that this rediscovery is actually happening, exactly as prophesized, and above all that I'm witnessing it. I am reassured that there is an intelligence, expressed in cycles and mathematics, behind what we call the universe.

All the current practitioners of the Toltec tradition, the Toltequity, must be embracing this shift, since we have had to wait for 500 years for the return of this wisdom. And now, witnessing the prophecies being fulfilled, we can be absolutely convinced of their veracity and accuracy.

Living in a world with the technology that will allow us to document these times in great depth, I can't help feeling curious about what will be added to the oral tradition to describe the current shift, especially since we know that not only has the Sun's transformation been chronicled throughout history, but so have the strengths and weaknesses of the people of the time.

I am extremely curious to know how the return of the feminine forces will affect us on social, political, and economic levels. I'm certain that a more equal, even matriarchal society will be created.

In addition to this, seeing all these changes has made me feel absolutely certain that I'm following the rhythm of the universe. I feel privileged to be here now and at the same time surprised by how the Toltecs and Aztecs were able to read what was written in the cosmos all those years ago.

The coming Sun is a time of great opportunity for spiritual growth on a personal level, especially compared to previous Suns. Its name and number indicate the return of the white Tezcatlipocas, the Quequetzalcóatl, those of precious knowledge. Though it may sound vain, why not think that we can be the beginning of the fulfillment of that prophecy?

Although there are 6,625 years for this to come to pass, we will begin now with an exercise to bring forth the Quetzalcóatl wisdom.

XAYAXOLOHTLI, XOLOTL'S MASK

Xolotl is Quetzalcóatl's *nahual*, a black dog who is in charge of taking us to the underworld.

If you do this exercise at midday, the time of Quetzalcóatl, you will be laying the foundations for your own Quetzalcóatl, your own enlightenment. If you do not get this far, you will be creating the basis for others to achieve it for the good of the planet.

❋ Sit down in a comfortable place, preferably facing east.

❋ Breathe in through your nose, filling your lungs to their full capacity. Hold your breath and visualize bringing energy up through your *totonalcayos* from your coccyx to your forehead in a serpentine movement. As the serpent moves upward, know that everything these centers represent is moving and helping you towards enlightenment.

❀ Once you reach your crown, turn left and remove all the negative energy patterns, the old Winds, that have accumulated there.

❀ Repeat this process 12, 25, 38 or 51 times, depending on how intense you'd like to make this exercise.

❀ The last time, repeat as before until you reach your crown. Then, blow the energy out, with all you've got, allowing it to shoot out of your head in the form of a serpent. This will transform into an eagle, which will soar into the sky, rising through the Winds, overcoming duality and the clouds, and freeing you of all your negativity, until it flies far beyond the moon, breaking the prison of the moon, and finally reaches a white sun. Once it is there, you will receive the sun's guidance in this new cycle.

❀ Put your hands together and say, "*Ometeotl*," and ask for the return of the Quequetzalcóatl to Earth. Then say again, "*Ometeotl*."

❀ At the end, count from one to four and come back to where you are.

These are interesting times we are living in. They are times of awakening, of revelation. I'll leave you with one final reminder of the young Cuauhtémoc's words: "Hide our treasure. Pass it from mothers to daughters, fathers to sons, teachers to students. Keep it safe, because it will be needed with the coming of the Sixth Sun."

May the glory and fame of Tenochtitlan prevail, the most majestic city of our time, where the strong Winds blow.

ABOUT THE AUTHOR

Sergio Magaña Ocelocoyotl is a well-known practitioner and teacher of the 5,000-year-old Toltec or Toltecayotl lineage of Mesoamerica. The tradition began with the ancient Chichimecas, who passed their knowledge to Teotihuacans and then the Toltecs, who then taught both the Mayans and Aztecs. Sergio is also trained in the Tol lineage of nahualism, dreaming knowledge that has been passed on in the oral tradition, without interruption, from master to student for 1,460 years. The time for these teachings to be unveiled is now, and Sergio is one of a few spokespeople asked to share this ancient and hidden wisdom with the world.

Sergio is the founder of Centro Energético Integral and the host of the radio show *The Sixth Sun*, which has aired in Mexico for 14 years. He speaks Spanish and English fluently, and has studied the mystical power of the Náhuatl language for many years. Sergio is a featured author in the book *Transforming Through 2012*, and author of *The Toltec Secret and Caves of Power*, both of which have been translated into numerous languages.

Sergio travels extensively and has a community of over 50,000 students in Mexico, the USA, Italy, the Netherlands, Sweden, Hungary, Canada, Spain and the UK. He lives in Mexico City and London.

www.sergiomagana.com

Hay House Podcasts
Bring Fresh, Free Inspiration Each Week!

Hay House proudly offers a selection of life-changing audio content via our most popular podcasts!

Hay House Meditations Podcast

Features your favorite Hay House authors guiding you through meditations designed to help you relax and rejuvenate. Take their words into your soul and cruise through the week!

Dr. Wayne W. Dyer Podcast

Discover the timeless wisdom of Dr. Wayne W. Dyer, world-renowned spiritual teacher and affectionately known as "the father of motivation." Each week brings some of the best selections from the 10-year span of Dr. Dyer's talk show on Hay House Radio.

Hay House Podcast

Enjoy a selection of insightful and inspiring lectures from Hay House Live events, listen to some of the best moments from previous Hay House Radio episodes, and tune in for exclusive interviews and behind-the-scenes audio segments featuring leading experts in the fields of alternative health, self-development, intuitive medicine, success, and more! Get motivated to live your best life possible by subscribing to the free Hay House Podcast.

Find Hay House podcasts on iTunes, or visit www.HayHouse.com/podcasts for more info.

HAY HOUSE
Look within

Join the conversation about latest products,
events, exclusive offers and more.

f   Hay House

   @HayHouseUK

   @hayhouseuk

   healyourlife.com

We'd love to hear from you!

Printed in the United States
By Bookmasters